CONVERSATIONS WITH LEW BINFORD

CONVERSATIONS WITH LEW BINFORD
Drafting the New Archaeology

By Paula L. W. Sabloff

With a postscript
by Jeremy A. Sabloff

UNIVERSITY OF OKLAHOMA PRESS
Norman

ALSO BY PAULA L. W. SABLOFF

(ed. with James Mauch) *Reform and Change in Higher Education: International Perspectives* (New York, 1995)

Will State Legislatures Increase Restrictions on Public University Autonomy? (Houston, 1994)

Library of Congress Cataloging-in-Publication Data

Binford, Lewis Roberts, 1930–
Conversations with Lew Binford : drafting the new archaeology / by Paula L. W. Sabloff ; with a postscript by Jeremy A. Sabloff.
p. cm.
Includes bibliographical references.
ISBN 0-8061-3008-3 (cloth) (alk. paper)
ISBN 0-8061-3059-8 (paper)
1. Archaeology—Methodology—History—20th century. 2. Binford, Lewis Roberts, 1930– . I. Sabloff, Paula L. W. II. Title
CC75.B49 1998
930.1—dc21 97–29892
CIP

Text design by Cathy Carney Imboden. Text is set in Berkeley Old Style Medium.

The paper in this book meets the guidelines for permanence and durability of the Committee on Production Guidelines for Book Longevity of the Council on Library Resources, Inc. ∞

1 2 3 4 5 6 7 8 9 10

Lovingly dedicated to
Joshua and Saralinda Sabloff,
who so enriched our adventures,
and to the memory of Tikal,
who learned "wolf" at the feet of the master

CONTENTS

List of Illustrations ix

Preface xi

[1] An Intellectual History of the New Archaeology 3

[2] Explaining the New Archaeology 39

[3] Antecedents: Early Influences 49

Postscript: The Intellectual Legacy of Lewis R. Binford, by Jeremy A. Sabloff 77

Appendix: A Brief Summary of Lewis R. Binford's Field Research 93

Select Bibliography of Lewis R. Binford's Works 99

Other Readings, Including Major Writings by Anthropologists and Archaeologists Mentioned in the Text 103

ILLUSTRATIONS

Illustrations following text page 70

Lew Binford with his parents

Binford at age ten or eleven

U.S. Army induction photo

Archaeological excavation, Roanoke River Basin, North Carolina, 1956

Binford at the Carlyle Reservation Project, Illinois, 1963

Binford in the Hunsgi Valley with K. Paddayya, 1986

Binford as Honorary Doctor of Letters, Southampton University, England, 1980

Binford and his wife, Nancy Medaris Stone, 1988

Binford and his daughter, Martha Binford, 1991

Binford with LuAnn Wandsnider and Robert Hitchcock, 1992

Binford with Luis Borrero, 1994

PREFACE

In 1982 I spent about six hours interviewing Lewis Binford in his office in the Department of Anthropology at the University of New Mexico. Since my husband, Jeremy Sabloff, and I had moved to Albuquerque (in 1978) and he had joined the department, we had become friends with Lew and his wife, Mary Ann. We spent many comfortable afternoons at their Corrales house, with Lew showing our young children his rabbits, turkeys, and sheep, and Mary Ann teaching them about the flowers and vegetables in her garden.

These visits would end with us sitting on the chaise lounges in the patio, sipping iced tea with a sprig of mint from the garden and discussing some issue of political or anthropological immediacy. I used to enjoy arguing with Lew just to see if I could hold my own for even a little while. Just when I felt backed into a corner, I would say, "But, Lew, how are you defining this term?" He would tell me, and I would reply, "Oh, I was defining it differently; we are really on the same side." And we would both be content to go on to another subject.

Why would Lew argue with me—a sociocultural anthropologist who had been trained in archaeology on the undergraduate level—in the first place? Only Lew can answer that; but I think that his mind craves constant stimulation, and he will talk with whoever is handy. He needs intellectual challenge the way all of us need water to replenish our bodies; it is that essential to him.

It was clear to me that Lew has an active mind coupled with a high level of curiosity. Any situation became a learning opportunity for him. My husband and I had proof of this one day while Lew was visiting in our kitchen. We had recently acquired a puppy, a cross between a Labrador retriever and an Irish setter, whom we named Tikal. Lew informed us that while he was doing fieldwork in Alaska, he taught himself "wolf" by listening to the cries of these animals during that field season. "Sure," we said skeptically. He replied, "Let me show you." He looked Tikal in the eye and began to howl. The poor puppy went skittering out of the room with his tail between his legs, clearly cowed. The next minute, Lew barked quietly, and Tikal came and put his head in Lew's lap. Lew alternately howled and barked softly, causing the poor animal to retreat and advance depending on the call. "Okay," we agreed, "You have, indeed, learned wolf."

The more I knew Lew, the more I wondered how he had come to challenge the entire archaeological establishment and develop the New Archaeology. Why did he do it? What did he not like about archaeology when he studied it? Where did he get the strength of character to buck an entire discipline—the one in which he planned to earn his living? Who influenced his intellectual growth? Who stimulated the new approach that he proposed for archaeology?

I decided to interview him in order to find answers to these questions. My plan was to use parts of the transcription of the interviews for an article in a popular science magazine. Lew agreed to the interviews, understanding my goal.

I never submitted the article to a magazine, one reason being that the editor of *Science '82* informed me that he never accepted a biographical article written by a friend of the subject. Since this initial, discouraging experience, I have been looking for the right place to publish the interviews. Hoping to keep them as close to the original as possible, I decided that they should stand on their own merit: they allow the reader to learn Lew's answers to the questions posed above. In this sense, the reader must remember that the book is more autobiography than history.

In chapter 1, Lew reminisces about his graduate years and describes how his intellectual development was stimulated by various institutions, faculty, and fellow students. In recounting his graduate training at the University of Michigan and his first teaching assignment at the University of Chicago, Lew brings to life the context in which the New Archaeology was developed as well as his view of its historical development. He discusses the Darwin Centennial, the differences between Leslie White and Julian Steward, as well as the place of Walter Taylor, Albert Spaulding, François Bordes, Robert Braidwood, and James B. Griffin in the development of the New Archaeology. Lew's description of these years allows the reader to understand his relationship to the growth of modern archaeology.

Chapter 2 is Lew's description of the New Archaeology and its evolution from the late 1950s to the time of the interview, 1982. This conversation lays out the key concepts behind his concerns about archaeology. Because he was not talking to a professional archaeologist, his explanations are in plain language, not the formalized language used in some of his scholarly works.

In chapter 3, Lew explains the early influences on his intellectual and emotional life—his parents and other family members; the Boy Scouts; and a very special teacher, Mrs. Henning. The foundations for the New Archaeology were laid during this period—Lew's youth, college years, and military service. It is clear that the strength of Lew's convictions began to develop at an early age.

I have preserved the tone of the interviews by keeping the transcription as close to Lew's actual words as possible. Once in a while his speech becomes ungrammatical, as happens to all of us when speaking extemporaneously; and sometimes Lew's mind races well ahead of his words—new ideas may suddenly enter a sentence in midstream. I hope that those who know Lew will actually be able to hear his speech patterns as though he were talking directly to them. Any omissions, due to minor editing or my inability to understand the tape recording, are indicated by ellipsis points.

The original interviews were more like conversations than interviews—free to wander when an important idea was raised. I felt that some of the material needed to be rearranged so that all the ideas about the New Archaeology would appear in one chapter and so that Lew's life story would retain chronological continuity. Due to this slight rearrangement, my original questions sometimes needed clarification, and so I changed some of my own words. I did not alter Lew's words without informing the reader, unless it was to make the grammar understandable. Any phrases or words that I added are in brackets.

What excited me in conducting these interviews was Lew's unraveling of his story—his personal development as a scholar and how he came to challenge the entire field of archaeology. Lew Binford is widely regarded as a seminal thinker, the man who pushed archaeology off the path of culture history and onto the path of scientific scholarship. These interviews offer Lew's insights into how he became that person.

The conversations are followed by Jeremy A. Sabloff's historical evaluation of Lew's contribution to archaeology along with lists of his publications and fieldwork and a section of suggested readings by anthropologists and archaeologists of note. These all give context to the interviews.

I would like to thank Lew for his help, encouragement, and friendship even though we have not been in touch since we all left New Mexico. Special thanks go to Nancy Medaris Stone, who has been important as a long-distance friend and the sheepherder of manuscript and photographs past Lew. I wish I could thank Mary Ann personally rather than posthumously, both for her insights into Lew and for her incredible example of modern womanhood. She had a full-time career in an area that made a tremendous contribution to young people's lives (among other things, she founded the kindergarten program in Albuquerque), was knowledgeable about her hobbies, and was an insightful and loving wife. She had kindness for everyone no matter what their age. Her untimely death hurt us all. Thanks also to Jeremy Sabloff, my husband, who made this project possible through his encouragement and contribution, and to Bill Woodcock, Merrilee Salmon, and Kathleen Allen, who read the initial manuscript and saw its merit. Finally, I would like to thank all the Mrs. Hennings of America, the teachers who saw more in us than we saw in ourselves. They made us better scholars as well as better people through their extra efforts.

PAULA L. W. SABLOFF

Philadelphia, Pennsylvania

CONVERSATIONS WITH LEW BINFORD

1

AN INTELLECTUAL HISTORY OF THE NEW ARCHAEOLOGY

Why did you develop the New Archaeology? Were you ever disgusted with old archaeology or was it a question of stimulation?

Initially, I kept saying, "What's wrong with me? There's got to be more to this than what I'm seeing. So there's something wrong with me." My assumption was that there had to be much more to the field than I as a student was seeing. There must be something wrong with my scholarship or whatever, or that I was dense, because I had had all this background in biology and other fields, really, and I kept looking for the complexities and I kept not seeing them in the literature. So I assumed, okay, this is a small field; argument is handled in face-to-face situations and meetings and so the literature is impoverished, not the field. And I kept looking for where the hidden complexities were and all the time basically learning that they were not there.

I went to college initially at VPI [Virginia Polytechnic Institute] in Virginia in wildlife management and wildlife biology. That is a technical school, so it has an enormous work ethic in the sense that it was a live-in school, a military school. We had these rigid schedules. You wouldn't believe the work schedule we had. I had this really rigorous background in math, biology, physics, chemistry, and all the basic natural sciences long before I ever even thought of going into anthropology. And when I went into anthropology, I kept looking for, Where are the roots? Where is the basis of this that we are all supposed to be doing? I kept initially questioning myself—"Well, I must be dumb, I can't see what is going on"—rather than getting upset about the field. Also I had a slightly different set of expectations because when I was in the military, I worked for some anthropologists as their interpreter, in Japanese. And so I got introduced to anthropology through ethnography.

I had this historical orientation out of biology—evolutionary. I wanted to know where forms come from, so once I began to see human societies like species—this one's different from that one; how did it get that way?—I sort of naturally moved to asking a historical question: How did this one get to be the way it is? And when I started reading—initially I went into anthropology to do ethnography, not archaeology—when I began to read ethnography, I realized that this is not going to work. The only primary record we have is archaeology, a social science. And all this culture-historical reconstruction stuff that you read from ethnography I did not think was very useful.

What time period are you talking about?

This was during the time I went to grad school [at the University of Michigan].

Who are you referring to?

[Alfred L.] Kroeber and all the classic anthropologists—that was the dominant thinking in ethnography when I went in. [A. R.] Radcliffe-Brown was talked about when I was a student—his functional approaches—but American archaeology was essentially historical reconstruction from ethnographic case material. It was not the more psychological stuff—I mean that was on the scene, culture and personality was there, but still the workhorse of American ethnography was trying to find out where the

Indians came from—[those] kinds of problems. So I became convinced that if we really want[ed] to know how these systems came into being, we would have to study the archaeological remains. Well, the irony was that what had led me to the conclusion that ethnography was not going to help was that [the ethnographers'] methods were not historical in fact. That is, you have to assume what you want to know in order to interpret the ethnographic record historically. And I went into archaeology, and what archaeologists were doing was using the methods of the ethnographers to make historical inferences. So right away I just rejected this—it was an intellectual thing that I thought was silly. If we are going to try to understand the past, we cannot do it with these conventions—that things that look alike must have common ancestors. Cladistic maps of culture based on simple measures of similarity and differences—I didn't think we could work that way.

But wasn't glottochronology valid?

I had studied glottochronology but I did not think it had any [validity]. . . . I just saw that as another silly example of the ethnographers' methods. Glottochronology did not work—there is no way to date a word. If you standardize [a word] on all your records, then, of course, it fits your data. You do not know whether it works on the cases you do not have control on or not. So it is like standardizing against a set of data, then it fits that data set. But the degree that it fits any others is not clear; it's taken on faith.

Anthropology always billed itself as a social science. So you entered anthropology expecting to study another science, again. Is that true?

Not really. I did not have a notion of science with a capital S. But I did expect the reasoning processes to not be tautological, and that you [would] be concerned with evaluating your ideas.

And what I found were all these conventions for interpreting things. You had to take the convention on faith and then everything fell into place. Like, how do you know whether migration occurred? The conventions were laid out very clearly in anthropology that if you had [trait] similarities appearing in a region that seemed to have no predecessors, then [the traits] had to be introduced. Now if there was a group of them [clusters of similar traits], then this meant that a group of people came in and brought a whole bunch of stuff along with them. On the other hand, if it was just one or two traits, then it was probably diffusion.

These were the conventions for interpreting the archaeological record, and in a sense you had your observations over here and your conventions over there. You just fit your observations to your conventions. Then you put them together. Your conventions literally gave conventional meaning to what you saw. And that was something that I was not willing to work with right from the very beginning. That seemed to me to be a truly alien way of thinking.

In the work that I had done as an undergraduate at VPI, almost every professor I had would have set this up as an example of prescientific thinking. It was shown to be the method of thinking in alchemy when we studied chemistry. This was the way they used to do it, and we do not do it that way any more. That was the kind of framework. I remember a course I had in developmental biology—in the development of biological concepts. We started with Carolus Linnaeus [1707–1778]. Well, the teacher lectured about Nils Ingebar (I think), who was Linnaeus's father. (They have a system in Scandinavia where you take your name from your mother.) It turned out that he, in fact, had written this huge, ten-volume treatise on plants and animals of the world. And he is Linnaeus's father, so obviously this is of interest. How did he classify the animals? He classified all the animals and plants in terms of the roles that they played in curing people. So you had all the plants that were thought to bring the *calor*—the heat—of the person. They were one kind of plant. And all the plants that caused coolness in people—they were another kind of plant. Then you had animals classified by the roles that they played in witchcraft. Frogs were used by black witches . . . so here is a whole system of classification in which the meaning given to the taxons is taken from the functions of that society. And here Linnaeus comes along and he says, "Look, this does not work—this is not the way to classify. We are going to take the strict morphology, and then the meaning of those things is not given by the way they are classified."

I can remember a long lecture on the difference between Linnaeus and his father in approaching biology. To me there was a clear analogy to the way in which lots of taxonomic classes were generated by anthropologists such that the meaning for the class literally was an ethnographic analogy to man's experience in the modern world. That, here is a scraper. Okay, I define a scraper in the following way. Therefore, that one over there is a scraper and that is what it was in the past. It is exactly like Nils Ingebar's reasoning about plants. I had had all this kind of stuff taught in biology and chemistry and physics at VPI, where we had a lot of history of ideas really taught. They would say, this is the way we did it in the Dark Ages, and this is the way we approach it now.

Physics was interesting—so was chemistry—because that era in the late '40s and early '50s was when there was a tremendous expansion in the number of elements thought to exist. I think when I started in school there were 89 elements, and when I finished there were 96. Now there are over 100.

One of the things that the teachers talked about was the impact of adding new knowledge where no new knowledge was thought needed. In other words, there is a big difference between recognizing that you are ignorant about something and seeking to correct it so you expect new knowledge versus a situation in which you think knowledge is self-contained—you do not need any more, and it comes to you anyway and impacts. They were forever using the implication of the recognition of the new elements in terms of the whole notion of compounds, you see. This seemed to be a really interesting intellectual thing to me. When I got into archaeology, I said, okay, all these people are saying all these little conventions—they are finite. They cover all the possible cases. It could be migration, it could be this, it could be that. Let us suppose we introduce a new possibility that nobody admitted to the system before, like functional variability. How would that impact all the other conventions? They all collapse really quick. They are not only redefined, but they basically collapse as a set of conventions because it is not just a convention of what the world is like; it is the conventions for identification, because you are dealing in archaeology with how you recognize something. So, if you admit that something else not included in the system is a possibility—that is, you admit ambiguity—then all your definitions are no longer finite; they all fall to pieces. That is really what—the way I had been trained to think about things, when I had gone to college initially.

Back to the years at Michigan:
Why did you question Julian Steward's approach?

Well, that wasn't me. I adopted [Leslie] White's criticism of Steward, I suppose. The most competitive people are the ones who do the most similar things. Since Steward was viewed by many Americans as advocating evolution, and so did Leslie White, of course the person that White criticized more [and] with greater interest and vehemence was Steward. And so Steward—Leslie's criticism of Steward was very instructive because it was the first time I had ever heard in anthropology a criticism that rang true in terms of the things I was talking about a minute ago. It sounded like what I had heard when I was in biology and physics. It was a criticism that was in terms of the logic and approach to learning rather than a criticism . . . that he didn't know this or he didn't know that. White's criticism of Steward was about how to do science. And that really rang with me; it impressed me.

So my reading of Steward. . . . Steward's anthology [*Theory of Culture Change*] came out in the '50s [1955]. It was not something that was available when I was a beginning student. I read it and discussed it during the time that I was a graduate student, I guess. He was at University of Illinois–Urbana. When his book came out, Leslie was all over it. We all had to read it, but we read it in the context of White's criticism. That really turned me on—White's criticism, verbally in class and otherwise, of Steward—because it was really the first time I saw anyone in anthropology talking about how to do science. And I liked that.

You had a special relationship with White?

It was the year of the Darwin Centennial [1959].* I spent a good part of that year in Chicago because Leslie [White] was very active in that and his wife was ill in a Chicago hospital. He did not know how to drive. So I was White's driver; I drove him back and forth between Ann Arbor and took him everywhere in Chicago at the Darwin Centennial.

What did they do for the Darwin Centennial?

Oh, my God. For the centennial, Chicago brought every person ever heard of including Darwin's offspring, [Thomas] Huxley, et

* See Sol Tax (editor), *Evolution after Darwin: The University of Chicago Centennial* (1960) for the papers presented during the centennial celebration.

cetera, and anybody who was doing basic research that could in any sense be said to be a derivative of Darwin's ideas—so it was all on the evolution of modern man. So it was all these Old World people that were researching—[Louis B.] Leakey and all his bunch—and all the people who were doing research on human evolution were all brought to Chicago for the Darwin Centennial. It went on for weeks with endless press releases, and newspaper [coverage], and television appearances, and debates, and all the religious people had to get their act in and come up and have debates with Huxley and Charles Darwin II. It was a show.

And White was involved in this very, very heavily. He gave his Sputnik speech there, which hit every newspaper in the country. Within weeks there were bomb threats and they tried to blow his house up in Ann Arbor. He said that he thought it was not an accident that the only modern nation to officially disclaim God as part of their political structure was the first nation to put up Sputnik. He did this in the context of arguing about the relationship between religion and technology—what causes culture change. Well, my God, every newspaper in the country: "University of Michigan professor says godless communism will succeed because. . . ." And so every fundamentalist outfit in town was sending bomb threats. It was astonishing.

Anyway I was his driver. It takes about six to seven hours to Chicago. Mary [White] all during this time was deathly ill with cancer in the hospital in Chicago. So he was going back and forth not only for the Darwin Centennial but because of her illness. She then died there. White's presence—I met all of the great men, literally; and most of them were still alive [at that time]. I met Kroeber; I spent hours listening to him and Leslie talk. This kind of stuff. It was a tremendous thing. White introduced me to all kinds of people at the conference.

I have never heard of Fay-Cooper Cole, even though I was an undergraduate major and started grad school in archaeology. And yet you talk about him a lot.

Yeah. As I had learned archaeology, Fay was basically said to be the man who started "modern archaeology" in that he tried to develop—he took the first steps of which Spaulding was still taking. That is, how you record the archaeological record in an accurate way rather than impressionistically. How do you excavate so as to see what you are digging through rather than just dig for things? All of these major changes in field method were basically referable to Fay-Cooper Cole; I mean he started them all, most of them.

He started this as a program out of Chicago in about 1928 with the experimental fieldwork in the upper Illinois Valley—'27 to '28. They learned an awful lot about how to dig. Almost all of the people who later ran the WPA projects* were trained by Cole in the '20s. So Cole's techniques became the standard for good archaeology during the WPA [era]. Some really incredible work—like that done by Madeline Kneberg, and [David] DeJarnette's excavations in Alabama, which are still superb—were done in terms of standards that were being discussed and pioneered by Fay-Cooper Cole in the Upper Valley in the '20s.

Almost all of in a sense putting American archaeology on a methodological footing was started by Fay-Cooper Cole. Everybody who thought of themselves as increasing the methodological skill of archaeology saw the history of it in terms of Cole and his training and his influence, and it continues into the present. I thought of myself that way in several ways. First, I thought of trying to continue the progress. Almost all of the

* Work Projects Administration, 1935–1943. The WPA was a New Deal agency that undertook extensive building, artistic, and educational projects, including archaeological excavations, during the depression.

people that I had worked with were trained by Cole. Joffre [Coe]* in [North] Carolina had been trained by Cole. [James B.] Griffin had worked for Cole. [Albert] Spaulding had worked under the WPA people who had worked for Cole. Everybody I had ever known in archaeology traced their lineage to Fay-Cooper Cole.

When I went to Chicago, it was the great romantic thing. When Cole left, they had a short period in which they tried to continue their archaeological program, and then they had done away with New World archaeology at Chicago after the war. They had given all the collections away—to Angel Mound [Indiana]—so that they had no program to offer in archaeology. Mainly the idea to reinstate the New World archaeology program was a function of Fred Eggan; he decided that they should have this in the curriculum. I was hired literally to sit in Fay's chair at Chicago, in that position. I felt that I had to live up to things. They treated me that way because there was a lot of stuff of his that was still around the department, and people when I came there dug it all out and brought it to me and said, "Maybe you can use this; this was Fay's."

I still have lots of Cole's stuff, some of which was given to me at the time I went to Chicago. More than that, I learned a lot about the man because there were all these files that had been packed up and stored in the old Walker Museum and when I came, everybody said, "These are things that belong in the New World program." Most of what they were [were] exams that Fay-Cooper Cole had given his students. You list the students:

* Stanley South says Coe, his and Binford's main anthropology professor at the University of North Carolina, taught them to question everything and everyone in archaeology. By teaching them to be highly critical, Coe implanted in Binford and South a desire to prove that they could do better archaeology or anthropology (personal communication, June 25, 1995).

Florence Hawley Ellis, I read all of her exams; read all of Ralph Linton, Fred Eggan—I read all of their exams. It was an incredible list. It was like *Who's Who* and there were all the files for them. I could see quite concretely the impact of this man on the field in a way that you don't see just anecdotally. All the students he had were 90 percent of the teachers who were out there.

Who were other influences on your graduate work?

In a sense, White was my philosophical model, and Spaulding was a methodological model, and Griffin became increasingly the challenge. That is, Griffin represented what an archaeologist did. And if you adopted the philosophy of White and the methods of Spaulding, how could you listen to Griffin, in a sense? So that Griffin—and I'm using this metaphorically because it was not just Griffin personally, it was the literature of the field—Griffin was the best spokesman at Michigan for the literature of the field.

Was this the culture history literature?

Yeah. If you adopt the philosophy that I already had and as it was modified for anthropology by White and the methodological approaches of Spaulding, then there was no fit to what was being advocated by Griffin and culture historians doing archaeology. Because there was no way you could take the philosophy on this hand and the methodology on the other hand and get the actual practicing archaeology out of either one of them, if you see what I'm saying.

Yes. Let's talk about Albert Spaulding.

Spaulding is interesting because there is a little bit of irony in Spaulding in that Spaulding is probably one of the smartest men I have ever known, and he has all this interest in physics. He reads chemistry for relaxation and this kind of stuff. I could talk to Spaulding. He would come in and be all turned on by something he had read in the latest journal of electrical engineering, and he did this. I mean he had these hobbies. He had an incredible breadth of interest in science—the natural sciences—so that talking with Spaulding was something very easy, in that sense, from my background—something that appealed to me.

The Spaulding-Ford debate was something I had had to read before I went to Michigan. He had had a debate with Jim Ford in the literature about how to type—whether you *discover* or whether you *invent* pottery types.* This was back to the Linnaeus argument, and that was something I was comfortable talking about. So when I got to meet Spaulding, it was really interesting. And the irony: I adopted his tactics. I believed what he told me about how to go about discovering artifact types and I worked like mad on it; I edge-punched cards in the early days of computers, where you had key sorters and all this kind of stuff, trying to do attribute analysis as Spaulding proposed.

And what I found was initially very disturbing. That is, instead of finding—if I studied projectile points—instead of finding projectile point types, what I almost inevitably found was that attributes didn't covary. In other words, if I studied length and width and the shape of the notch and the shape of the base, instead of finding some points that had a set of those things associated [with them] and [were] distinct from another group of points that had a different and distinguishable set, what I most of the time found was that each one of those things varied independently and crosscut one another. And I couldn't see any sets. So for a long time I thought this was because of what I had chosen

* See Gordon Willey and Jeremy Sabloff, *A History of American Archaeology* (1993: 164–169) for further explanation of this debate. They write, on page 165, "In this debate, Ford championed the type as an imposed or designed construct of the archaeologist; A. C. Spaulding led the attack on behalf of those who saw it as discovered."

by accident to study—that Spaulding had to be right, and I had just chosen something that was unique, but his principles were correct in other ways. I still continued to try to do this [attribute analysis], and the more I did this, the more I found that each time I studied something in more and more detail, instead of things getting clearer, they got more and more detailed.

Patterns weren't coming out?

No, there was just more variability, which I didn't understand. So instead, when I did these pattern recognition studies, what I found was there were more and more facts, and none of those enlightened the ones that I was interested in when I started. Each exercise impressed me that my ignorance was greater than I had imagined, and the exercise did not increase knowledge; it just increased my appreciation of my ignorance.

So at that point, I said, look, these procedures aren't going to help us—that is, the taxonomic procedures, the approaches to pattern recognition—the seeing-the-world-more-clearly approaches—which were really the approaches that Spaulding and others were playing with in an attempt to answer Walter Taylor.

Taylor said, "There's more things to be seen than we are seeing. The past was full of vibrant life and all we are talking about is stupid chronology. We should be able to get more out of the archaeological record."

Well, Spaulding in a sense was one of the few who was trying to explore ways of doing that in a very systematic, methodical fashion. I adopted his procedures and did these things. Finally, the bell rang: the procedures don't give me meaningful statements, they just give me more and more facts of the archaeological record.

The interesting thing is that I began to know that in Ann Arbor by 1958. But I saw it as unique to what I was studying. I didn't generalize it to the field until 1968, on the Mousterian problem. That is, that if you had a problem in archaeology—and I had

[François] Bordes's Mousterian type, he's observed this pattern—you've got four different kinds of types. That by going and studying more properties of the archaeological record* that somehow or another I wasn't going to clarify the properties that already had been described. I still believed that until 1968: that if you've got a problem, the solution rests in studying more completely the archaeological record. You see what I'm saying?

Yes; in other words, you as the investigator are missing something.

That's right. So what you do is go look for more things—open up bigger eyes. The analogy was that, look at all the wonderful things that would. . . . [That was] the analogy that I used to use—I even used it in print when I talked about doing a factor analysis. Doing a factor analysis, I said, was like inventing a microscope. You bring a new technical device to bear, and you can see whole domains that you could not see before. The whole challenge of knowing more about the past rested with our ability in a sense to make bigger and bigger eyes. And so that was the whole early thrust. In that, I followed Spaulding's footsteps.

Didn't attribute analysis work in pottery?
There you had these clear patterns popping out at you.

No, you didn't. I would disagree with you in the following sense. If you already had a bunch of pottery types and you said, "I want to verify my intuitive feelings through attribute analysis," and then you objectify the attributes that you had used to separate them

* François Bordes pioneered a new quantitative methodology that helped him define four types of Mousterian tool assemblages. He attributed these types to four different ethnic groups. Binford argued not with Bordes' methodology but with his interpretation. Lew and Sally Binford contended that the four types reflected functional differences in tools related to variable adaptive behavior. See Binford, *In Pursuit of the Past* (1983: chap. 4) for further explanation.

in the first place, then, yes, they are very separate. But if you went and said, "I'm just going to take the pottery [and analyze it using the strategies of traditional typologists]," it was not approaching it the way Spaulding advocated.

I have done attribute analysis so it comes out. But it was done to verify judgments made in more traditional typologies. It was not approaching it the way I was with the projectile points and saying, "Okay, we have to be completely 'objective' in the old sense of the word. Here are all the properties that I can think of that a projectile point can have. Now let's look at how they distribute when I look at cases." And what I found was that they varied independently of one another: crosscut, complicated, convoluted patterns that made the intuitive types no longer quite so clearly defined, because there were all these cross-cutting categories and things.

What body of data were you working on?

I was working mainly on projectile point types from the Great Lakes, Archaic projectile points.

You know where I keep getting lost? I keep getting lost in Spaulding's methodology. Well, he was doing attribute analysis, you're saying.

That's right.

And then you're saying that you wanted to adopt that—to use it—and now you're telling me you rejected it.

That's right.

You tried it and then rejected it?

Well, not initially. I just kept saying, "Well, it probably works somewhere else, but my little experience was bad." So I still continued to believe that we could clarify the past by, in a sense, clearing up the glasses through which we look at the archaeological record. I did not really realize that the problem of knowing the past is not a problem of looking but . . . a problem of thinking. And it was not until later that it really became clear that a knowledge of the past is a function of how you justify the meanings you give to the archaeological record; it is not a function necessarily of how we look at it. In other words, no matter how I look at it, I still have the intellectual task of assigning meanings to what I've seen, what I am finding. And so the big problem for archaeology is the latter, that is, How do we go about giving meaning to what we have seen? And I guess I knew that intellectually, but I still was following the other procedure for so long.

And that was true even in the early days at Chicago, because when I talked to my students there about changing archaeology and making it—doing process and all this—all of us were really oriented toward cleaning up the archaeologist's act: doing better fieldwork, doing more comprehensive kinds of record keeping, digging better, making better records of excavation. If we did that, then we were going to describe the archaeological record more accurately and therefore we would have a more accurate past. All the time we were doing this, the whole role of theory kept coming in, but I never really dealt with it very systematically, I fear, until after 1968. I mean I was aware of it, and all the arguments I made about how to argue from analogy and all this—I saw it as a problem. But I saw this as an abuse, not the central problem. It was an abuse of what we saw, not the central problem of dealing with it—until after about 1968.

What happened in 1968?

Total frustration. That was when Sally [Binford] and I went to France to work on the data that Bordes was going to make available to me. The same facts that he had [derived] his four tribes from, we were going to go over it, with full cooperation, to see if we couldn't use the same facts to prove that there were not four tribes, or whatever. So, my God, we studied everything you can imagine—tabulated everything. I still have reams of stuff back there [in his back office room] of new facts we generated about the Mousterian. But none of them whispered in my ear. Instead of clarifying things, what I came around to was realizing how much incredible ignorance we had—more ignorance. I came back with more ignorance than I went away with.

At that point, that was literally when I finally faced the issue, okay, that the archaeological record is static. It does not talk; it just sits there. It is contemporary. All my observations are in the *present*. They are not observations on the past; they are observations that I make in the present. And so if I am going to make any statements about the past, and those statements are about dynamics—are about events—then it is a problem of inference. And so the central problem is one of inference justification: not how to look but how to justify saying anything about what you have seen.

How is that any different from the old archaeology in the long run? That is very pessimistic—what you're saying.

No. It's very optimistic. Why? Because the old archaeology said they knew what it all meant. There was a series of conventions that when you see this, it means that, and most any of those conventions could be knocked down. This is what we did in the early '60s: show you that there are three or four different ways that you could get the same patterning. That was what my earliest argument was all about—that I could invent a scenario that, if it had been true, would account for the same facts that traditional archaeologists are confidently saying mean one thing; and—if my scenario was plausible—[those facts] would mean something totally different!

Spaulding again:

Why was what Spaulding was doing not the New Archaeology?

Because Spaulding was simply asking for more rigor in the conceptual tools for doing old archaeology. He was very comfortable sliding into the New Archaeology later on, but at that point he was not doing—he was not worrying about the justifications for giving meanings to things. He was just worrying about the criteria for pattern recognition in the archaeological record.

The New Archaeology was not developed in a vacuum. Before proceeding with the development of the concept, I'd like to explore the context in which you were beginning to rethink archaeology. Let's go back to the '50s and your undergraduate years at the University of North Carolina a little bit more. What were your fellow students doing? Was there any intellectual stimulation from them?*

Yeah. Stanley South was one; he worried about archaeology with me [at the University of North Carolina]. That was before I went to Michigan. He had also come into archaeology from a totally [different background]. He had been a high school science teacher—taught chemistry and physics and biology—and had been fired from the Goldsboro, North Carolina, school district for teaching evolution. He took it to court and won and then resigned and decided to come back to school and do what he always wanted to do and that was archaeology. His motives were romantic, I think. He had collected arrowheads as a kid, and he always wanted to know what the past was like. His background was in science itself. He was an older fellow and so was I. At

* After undergraduate work at VPI and a stint in the army, Binford completed his B.A., in anthropology at the University of North Carolina–Chapel Hill (1956). He went to graduate school at the University of Michigan from 1956 to 1960, began teaching at the University of Chicago in 1961, and received his Ph.D. from the University of Michigan in 1964.

North Carolina, we talked a lot about science and archaeology and that sort of thing. So Stanley South was really important.

Right off the bat, he and I both came in conflict with another student, John Grant. He was a student of Margaret Mead's in ethnography and had done his undergraduate work at Columbia [University] and worked with Mead and all this [Erik] Erikson/Mead business in culture and personality. He was forever pushing that this was the way to go. Stanley and I—coming out of a natural science background—just listened to this as gobbledegook. So right away in our little group, we had a series of support and conflict positions. Most of the time, Stanley and I were able to make mincemeat of John Grant. So this reinforced us that we were right, though it probably had nothing to do with being right, but it reinforced us.

By the time I went to [the University of] Michigan, where there was a strong materialist bias, I was all ready to listen to every word of it because Stanley and I had already successfully argued for that position in our own little student group, that is, amongst ourselves. So I was all ready to listen to anything materialist that came down the path at that point. At Michigan, there were some graduate students who were important—Bobby Joe Williams was a physical anthropologist. He worked [on] hunters and gatherers, and he teaches at UCLA [the University of California at Los Angeles]. He was a close friend and a good thinker and someone that I could try out ideas on and talk to.

There was an army colonel by the name of Drexel Barney Cochran that the air force had sent back to school to get a degree. He was a jet ace from Korea. Barney—before he went into the military—had been in anthropology and kind of had a romantic notion of Southeast Asia, had this love for Fay-Cooper Cole's work in the early days in Sumatra and Southeast Asia. Barney was all into hunters and gatherers. He was really interested in them, why I do not know. He was forever—whenever we would take ethnography courses—trying to say, "Look, the one thing you have to understand if you are going to do evolution is the form that came before the form you are interested in. If you're interested in agriculture, you have to know hunters and gatherers. And no matter what, if you are interested in complex societies, you have to know horticulturalists." In a sense I think Barney was right. I became more and more interested in hunter-gatherers largely because of him as an archaeologist. And he impacted, oddly enough, Bobby Joe Williams. He studied hunter-gatherers in Southeast Asia. And I think Barney had a lot to do with this.

Barney was a character. Oh, my God, he was a classic Terry-and-the-Pirates type with his hat on the side, and he talked out of the side of his mouth. But he was a smart fellow and had a lot of interesting experiences and had a great deal of impact. He organized us, essentially. You know that among graduate students there is always one who organizes. Barney had lots of money. None of us had money. So he could have us over to his house all the time and it was no sweat off his monetary back. Barney was important in our little student group at Michigan. Certainly his interest in hunter-gatherers rubbed off on me.

Who were you living with? Did you live as a group? I mean, how did you influence each other's thinking?

I was married to Jean Mock [until I left Michigan]. When I first went to Michigan, the cheapest house I could get was out in Dexter, Michigan. It was eighteen miles from Ann Arbor on a little lake. Bobby Joe got a similar deal on another lake, twenty-four miles across distance this way. Basically, we were allowed to live in the houses to take care of them. They were summer homes of wealthy people, and we would live in them in the winter. There was very little graduate student life [for me while] living in Dexter except what happened on campus, so I was anxious to move into Ann Arbor. There was a politically left organization in Ann Arbor that I was conversant with that got enough money together to buy a building and have a co-op apartment building. I was all due to move in there and went to move and found out there was one man in line ahead of me—Art Saxe. Art Saxe was then a beginning student in vocational education. He wanted to be a shop teacher and go back to the Bronx to teach the heathens how to progress. I met Saxe because he got the apartment that I thought I was to have in the communist co-op in Ann Arbor and [so I] began to know more about the people who were living in that outfit.

Through some of them I found a house of a person who was politically left and was willing to let people rent it for practically nothing because he didn't care. I went into this house. It was actually four houses around a court. I lived in one. Jules Dassin's son, Joe Dassin, lived in another one—we had all of the movie people on one side, and the first foreign students from the Caribbean that came on a cultural enrichment program lived in a co-op on the other side, and a homosexual ecologist lived in the fourth home. This was quite a group. Joe Dassin, his group, and his sister Julie lived in one place with all the left-wing politicos from the movie world. Art Saxe and I had the anthro house, and then there was the Caribbean steel band group, and then the homosexual ecologists. This is where I lived the rest of the time I was in Ann Arbor

Whenever one would have a party, everyone came. You must realize it was corporate living. And in fact we used to hold classes down there—Jim Spuhler taught there. I held seminars down there. Spuhler used to come down and hold his classes there. We did it because if we got to talking, no one would turn the lights out on [us], and we could have beer. We held lots of course work down on Whaley Court. It was very close to campus—only a block and a half from the main campus. It's torn down now.

Did you get any support from faculty at Michigan?

Most of the [intellectual] support came from Spaulding, on the one hand, and the ethnographers, on the other. Not from Griffin or Emerson Greenman. Griffin was tremendous [in other ways]. He . . . got me jobs and kept me employed. He made opportunities open up. But intellectual support came from people like David Aberle, Elman Service, Leslie White. Fred Thieme was in physical anthropology, and he was very active in experimental research. The field of physical [anthropology] in his sense [of the term] was already into testing ideas and justifying your inferences. I remember Thieme was worrying on how you can tell sex from a skeleton. He was dealing with ambiguity of recognition, which is something archaeologists were not dealing with, or not recognizing as a problem. Or you took someone's judgment as being the best evidence—that person's authority.

Aberle I suppose was the first—Aberle actually supported me. I worked once for Aberle. I ran down all of his Navajo early records from the Indian agencies all across the Southwest on the Navajo reservations. He hired me to work for him. There was support outside of . . . and there was a kind of joking relationship. That is why Barney [Cochran] was important. He was there as an ethnographer, but his interest in hunter-gatherers got all of these archaeologists interested. So the ethnographers in the context of talking about hunter-gatherers all of a sudden found they had something to say to the archaeologists, which is something that had never happened before.

How did you switch to the Old World? You started in the New World. How did Bordes know to contact you?

Well, he didn't. When I went to Chicago [in 1961], I was hired by [Robert] Braidwood mainly because I had some reputation [for] working on shell mounds. Braidwood had found shells at Jarmo [Iraq] and needed somebody who knew something about shells. Technically, I was hired as a New World archaeologist at Chicago. I had originally always wanted to work on Old World—on human evolution from earliest material. I had been discouraged from this—was told I did not have any independent wealth and could not do it without independent wealth. I always worked on local projects and by default had become a New World archaeologist because that's where I was. And . . . I went to Chicago because I was hired to teach North America—that was my job. Of course everybody there was interested in Old World, which was new for me. In Ann Arbor, it was taught, but it was taught by Spaulding. There was nobody who was actively doing research.

Once I got to Chicago, I began really to be involved in Old World studies. Before, I had just read textbooks. But these guys were doing research and knew what it was all about. . . . There were others—at the Oriental Institute. I began to read the literature in a totally different way. I began to realize that it was not some unattainable moon. I knew these people and they were working in the Old World all the time. It was something that could be done. But the thing with Bordes was a little more because F. Clark Howell had brought Bordes to this country for the first time to lecture as a guest lecturer at Chicago. I met Bordes then for the first time in 1959, the year before I went there to teach.

You started in the New World.
Now you've been all over. How did this happen?

I had always wanted to do Old World. I really wanted to research the evolution of man in a sense. So that whenever opportunity came, in spite of the fact that I did New World work, I read Old World work because I was interested in it. And by virtue of having knowledge of the literature, when opportunities came to argue about methodology, I included Old World as well as New

World; I wasn't provincial in that sense. And so when opportunities for doing research opened up in these areas, I would jump on them like a bug. I just tried to make them happen. The biggest single problem that seemed clear to me to address was the Bordes argument. And so, that was a methodological problem. It happened to be in the Old World, but it was basic, crucial, and so I began to work on that and continued to for a long while. And in the process of doing it, the crucial issue was, How do hunters and gatherers behave? So how you . . . you have to learn about hunter-gatherers. There are only so many places where they are still around.

So you adopted Patty-Jo [Watson]'s idea of ethnoarchaeology.

Yeah, but not her way of doing it. But, yes, that strategy.

I want to understand Bordes more.

That was the real first glimmering that I had that the problem was not how to look but how to think. In the sense that Bordes had done mainly the same thing—had been successful—in doing what Spaulding was trying to do with attribute analysis. Bordes had done it at the assemblage level and had been able to come up with a procedure that did not rest with somebody's opinion but was a procedure that gave you a result.

How did it differ from Spaulding?

Oh, a lot. Bordes was much more concerned with discovering assemblage types, not artifact types. He stipulated artifact types—mainly because he was so skilled at flint knapping that he just dismissed a lot of things as crap or meaningless and picked out attributes and then said, "This is meaningful, or will be meaningful, and we are going to do it this way." Then he looked at the first derivative effect, not at the types themselves but at the patterns—the interaction the types produced at the assemblage level. And he began to see different kinds of Mousterian.

Once he did this, he could see that the expectation that one should follow the other in an evolutionary sequence was physically not met in the archaeological record—that you get one type, then you get another type, then you get the first type again, chronologically. This seemed to be from my perspective the first time that you had a clear challenge to a clear set of expectations. In other words, here the archaeological record had a voice—it was talking back. It was saying, "I'm not the way you think I am." That, of course, in any science is the most exciting thing that can happen because it tells you that your knowledge is inadequate. The first step is being able to in a sense give a voice to the facts, design a set of methods so that the facts can speak back to you so it is not a tautology, it is not a closed system of reason; and then to be able to go to the empirical world and in fact have the facts tell you, gee, your ideas are inadequate. Now you know you have gotten a chance to learn something. . . . When I first heard about the Bordes situation, [it was] the most exciting thing that I could see in the field because of this. That is, the expectation that culture should proceed from preceding cultural forms through a directional sequence in the stratigraphy was not met in these facts. So that all the expectations—intuitive or whatever, a theoretical bent—all archaeologists would expect that culture proceeds from preexisting forms, so that if I have got Culture A here, then what is on top of it should be some modified derivative, and then the next one should not be like what was down here but should be like what was immediately preceding it. Everybody believed that.

That was not what Bordes was finding. He was finding this alternation of industries. He got Type A and then Type B and then Type A again. Then Type C and Type A again, et cetera. There's no directionality to this sequence of assemblage forms through a deposit. I was attracted to that from pure intellectual stimulation. It wasn't linked to my desire to be an Old World archaeologist. It was linked to my instinct [regarding] what situations signal a potential learning situation. When I met Bordes I immediately started arguing with him and found him really interesting because if you just listened to [Hallam] Movius about the tribes, it sounded like Bordes just believed this out of the blue. But when [I] talked to Bordes, what I found out was that Bordes had already thought of all the things I had thought of. He said, Was it seasonal variability? And he had rejected this because he could not find any reason to believe it. Is it structural poses of a system going through some kind of seasonal round? The answer is no. Is it response to environmental differences? Answer: no, because there is no correlation between the form and the type of the environment. And he had already done all of this, you see. He was not some dumbbell just asserting that this is what the world was like. He had gone through all of the logical alternatives available to him and had concluded that the only model that fit the case was tribes migrating in and out and their cultures not changing.

All right. So this is the idea of the tribes.

Yeah. Movius basically accepted that argument, and he presented the Mousterian model in terms of Bordes's conclusions.

Movius interpreted Bordes for America?

Yeah. An important article—this is probably the best article that Movius ever wrote—and it was the introduction of the Bordes system to New World people, and here it is. Here's the history of the French system, and then you see him in Movius's article [1953] in Kroeber's volume explain the whole Bordian system in here. Here's Bordes's system being explained by Movius to New World people. And nobody had ever heard of Bordes before this article and before F. Clark Howell began to push. Howell learned about Bordes from Movius. This was certainly the most influential article of its time. That was where I learned about Bordes—from Movius's article.

I went to France to see Bordes first in '64. I went at Christmastime because I wanted to see the materials. I had never really seen the Mousterian. I received financial aid from Wenner-Gren to go during the Christmas holiday to see Bordes and to look at the Mousterian. School was closed for him, but he came in and opened up the whole lab, and he let me do anything I wanted to and whatnot. I went again in 1966 because by that time I had done computer work on his tabulations and wanted to—no, he came to this country again and stayed at my house in Chicago, and that's where we went over the first computer stuff. Then he said, and I had done the Jabrud [Syria] stuff, which Sally and I published in '66—he then said, "Well, why don't you two try the Combe Grenal [France], the biggie?"

I said, "Marvelous!"

He said, "Well, you can come and get the data yourself." Sally and I first worked on Combe Grenal in '66 and then went back in '68—spent the whole year there working on Combe Grenal. That was when I did endless cross-tabulations. I finally realized why I wasn't succeeding. I still was operating as if the facts somehow would clarify themselves, and each time I had a problem I sought more facts. I got more facts, and the result was that I simply realized that there were a lot more things that I did not understand than I started with.

Were you at Chicago then?

I was in California then. Actually, we [Sally and I] were coming here [to New Mexico] then. We had gotten money to go to France and [Jack] Campbell had contacted me about coming here. I said, "I'll come if you will let me have a leave the first year because I already have the money to do fieldwork." That was '68. "I'll come and start teaching in '69." They said that would be all right. Instead of getting the grant through the California system, I got it through New Mexico and had my first year at New Mexico on leave in France.

Why is New Archaeology associated with your name when you say that there was a group of you at Chicago?

New Archaeology was associated with my name because I think I wrote the articles that people read and saw as the intellectual changes, or arguments for change. I think that was generally true throughout. I had a lot of students who wrote articles, but in general, in one way or another, they were following up things that I had already put into print, or argued for at national meetings.

In Chicago, what were these students doing before you came to teach? Who were your students studying with before you came to teach? Why were they so eager to join you?

I don't know other than that while I was at Chicago we did a lot of team-taught teaching. For instance, we taught a two-semester course called "The Human Career" in which Braidwood, Clark Howell, Bob [Robert McC.] Adams, and I all taught, plus usually a visitor. One year it was Bordes; one year it was Alberto Blanc, Carl-Axel Moberg, [J.] Desmond Clark. So there [were] usually five faculty teaching that course. My teaching responsibility—in a funny sense—overlapped. I was supposed to handle the New World and of course Clark Howell was the early time ranges and hunter-gatherers in Europe. Then Braidwood was supposed to get them all sedentary, and Adams was supposed to make them complex. Well, I was supposed to do the things of antiphonal relevance in the New World. Where it was Pleistocene for Howell, it was hunter-gatherer for the New World. Where it was formative stuff relative to Braidwood, and then it was complex society. So Clark Howell would start the course, and then I would teach with him; and then he would drop out, and Braidwood would come. I would teach with him; and then Braidwood would drop out, and I would teach with Bob Adams. So the students saw me relative to the three teachers in this team-taught course, all the way through this required core course. And I guess my points of view were frequently argued, and we frequently argued with one another in front of the class. And I guess some students thought I was worthwhile.

Where do people like James Hill, Steve LeBlanc, Charles Redman, and Patty Jo Watson fit in?

Jim Hill was a student at Chicago in the second generation of my students there. Steve LeBlanc was an undergraduate at [the University of California at] Santa Barbara. Patty Jo Watson was different. She was a senior student finishing up her Ph.D. under Braidwood when I came to Chicago, so she had really pioneered the idea of doing ethnoarchaeology. She and a person by the name of Leshnick, who had done his degree with Braidwood on India. And these were the late '50s—they had done ethnoarchaeological work. I knew Patty in that context—as a senior student when I was a junior faculty at Chicago. In a sense she was a person that Braidwood tended to turn to to get things done. She was the reliable one on Braidwood's team

I didn't really see much of Patty until I was teaching at UCLA [1966–1967] and she and Red [Richard Watson—her husband] came through one day and said, "We're going to do this book on the New Archaeology," which sort of surprised me. Her husband has a degree in geology and one in philosophy. He thinks of himself as a philosopher of science. He had gotten interested in the literature of archaeology and was using it, and Pat in turn had a lot of philosophy input from her husband; so they—she had over the years gradually developed this course at Washington University in St. Louis that was really [on] the philosophy of archaeology, and it was the first time that anybody ever tried to do that. She was drawing on the arguments that I, too, and others were having as examples of philosophical argument. She had gone to the field with Braidwood in Turkey. [Charles] Redman was then a student of Braidwood—this was long after I had left Chicago—and LeBlanc for some reason was on that crew.

Patty Jo Watson got in touch with Redman and LeBlanc in the field under Braidwood in Turkey. Basically, I guess Redman took a course from Patty Jo; I do not know whether Steve [LeBlanc] did or not. In any event, they decided to write a book as a result of this interaction. Whether it was in class or in the field I'm not exactly sure. I had nothing to do with that. I never had Redman as a student. I never really had much interaction with Patty Jo except to acknowledge that she was my generation and she had done some interesting things in ethnoarchaeology. But I never had any direct interaction with them.

Who were your students? Who do you claim?

The group at Chicago: [Stuart] Struever, [Kent] Flannery, Henry Wright, Bob Whallon, Jim Hill, [William] Longacre, Leslie Freeman, a couple of linguists, Chris Peebles, John Fritz, Jerry Eck (studied primates)—that's mostly the Chicago group. The ones who worked the closest with me intellectually were probably Bob Whallon, Henry Wright, and Jim Hill—that is, in terms of arguing ideas and keeping any contact.

How did it happen in the early '60s that the New Archaeology was used as an epithet against you, and by '68, if you weren't a New Archaeologist, you could not get a job in the field? How did it switch so fast?

I don't really know. I thought it was silly because a lot of what was being called the New Archaeology—I didn't think they understood what I thought had to be done. The early days of argument were basically arguments showing that the methodology of archaeology is ambiguous and therefore limited. It was a negative thing—trying to show that this doesn't work, what people have been doing all along doesn't work very well. Obviously, if you are [going to] take this approach, which is a destructive approach, then the question you must face is, How do you put in place something that *does* work? I never claimed that I could answer that; yet the responses by the early '60s were by people who were saying there is a way. Well, I never knew what that way was. I'm just now beginning to see how to do it. But there was a—and it was almost an adopting, almost like a fad—you adopt sampling (which we had argued about as important); you adopt settlement pattern studies in broadscale research, large excavations, controlled surface collection—all these things that we had talked about being able to use in better equipping the archaeologist to describe the archaeological record.

But you see that wasn't what I was saying was the big problem. The big problem was, How do you give meaning to what you've seen after you've seen it? So, advocating all these ways of doing better fieldwork didn't solve the problem. For instance, I've seen articles from the Deep South saying, "I'm a New Archaeologist because I am doing a random sample." Basically, they're still talking technique. And it got to be such a social thing—I mean, it got to be vicious. I had been involved in one vicious scene that was largely over morals and ethics.

I basically pulled out. I stopped going to meetings; I resigned from the SAA [Society for American Archaeology]; I went into the field in 1969. It was not until [Jeremy] Sabloff came here [to the University of New Mexico] in 1978 that I decided to reengage in the field. I rejoined the SAA after Jerry came here. I hadn't been to a meeting since 1968 simply because in order to get done what I thought needed to be done, all that was crap. I didn't care what they thought. The arguments about choosing up sides—

who is right and who is wrong—there was no basis for making such a judgment because we didn't know how to use the archaeological record. There was a sociological flap that happened. If I encouraged it, I apologize. I don't think I encouraged it. It had nothing to do with what I was trying to do intellectually.

I'm sure. It's fascinating that a field could reverse so fast. Where was the old guard? Why couldn't it support its position? How did it fall apart so fast?

It fell apart because of demographic change. When I went to the national meetings in 1956 in Philadelphia, there were 230 people attending the annual meeting of the SAA. By 1970, the attendance must [have been] in the thousands. Just the rate of growth of the field was staggering. You see, as long as the only place you could get a job was Harvard, Michigan, Berkeley, UCLA, Chicago, and Yale, then the old guard controlled who got jobs. But when every university—good, bad, and indifferent—is adding archaeologists to their staff, the old guard can't control who gets jobs.

The same kind of thing was true with respect to funding. Now this is where some politics went on. When the National Science Foundation [NSF] was first put together, the advisory board deciding who got money [was made up of] the members of the National Academy of Sciences [NAS] in the field. In other words, the National Academy of Sciences was legally constituted to advise the United States government and the president on things scientific. When the National Science Foundation was reorganized (Spaulding was the first director of the anthropology program—in 1958), research funds were being made available for basic research. Before that it had all been done at the local level, and you did it on the weekend or you got some salvage money. There were no funds except for a little bit of money from the American Philosophical Society—it was two thousand dollars at most—or personal money. For the first time, archaeology had backing at the research level.

The first advisors were the members of the National Academy of Sciences, who were Irving Rouse, Hallam Movius, Emil Haury, and others. It was the power block of traditional archaeology. It was clear to me and others that as long as that was the case, no one had a chance to get any money. There was a big push politically made for the advisors to the director in the National Science Foundation not to be the members of the National Academy of Sciences but to be appointed by the executive committee of the Society for American Archaeology, which is a democratic institution, and you can participate in it in principle just by paying a fee. That worked. And that was the first time in a sense that the control of the old guard was broken.* Because all of a sudden there was a short time there when popularists' ideas were funded more than traditionalists' ones.

I haven't had any money from the National Science Foundation for ten years. I can't get any money from them because of the bullshit now. But for a while there it was easier probably for me to get money in the early, mid-sixties than it was for Jimmy Griffin.

Why can't you get it now?

Because there are all these people out there who don't even know what the world is like and they're just on ego trips. If they can criticize me, why then they're somehow great. It's just bullshit.

* This passage sounds as if the conversion from NAS advisors to SAA advisors was a formal arrangement. According to the present NSF director for archaeology, John Yellen, the advisory panel is selected by the NSF, not the SAA or NAS. Whereas Spaulding might have selected people who were members of the NAS, subsequent directors selected whom they wished. The fact that many members of the SAA have served on NSF advisory panels is a reflection of their professionalism rather than their membership (personal communication, John Yellen, July 2, 1995).

So where do you go for money?

I don't get any. I do it on my own. I haven't had any research backing from anywhere since about 1974.

But what about your Eskimo work?

That was financed. That was the last money I had; it was done between '69 and '73.

But you've gone into the field since then?

Yeah, but it's not been through normal funding. The Australian government paid me to come and do work in Australia; the UN [United Nations] paid me to come and do work in South Africa. I can't get any normal research money. It's pretty much a game.

When did you go to Australia?

In '74. After I had finished working in the Arctic. In '69 I went to the Arctic. I worked through '73 in the Arctic and then went to Australia in '74 and started that project—and my son, Clint, was killed in '74 and [so I] dropped [the project]. I saw a constructive direction for work but then I had to leave. By the time that I could have returned, [James] O'Connell had learned the language and moved the research in new directions.

In other words, you were invited by the Australian government to direct the project.

Or get things going. I was to create a project [concerning the ethnoarchaeology of an Aboriginal group], collaborating with Jim O'Connell. I went out and did get the project going. And then I had to leave [because of Clint's death]. And of course by the time that I came back they had all learned the language and were proceeding along different lines. Once I had left, I didn't have much input. My original plan was to collect data comparable to what I got in the Arctic. While O'Connell focused initially on site structure, he moved in the direction of researching optimal foraging theory. What O'Connell did was know something about what we were trying to accomplish and then improvise as he met new things.

When did you go to Africa?

In '80. I was invited by the government again to teach—you see, archaeology in South Africa is national—and to teach a series of seminars for archaeologists. The South African funds made it possible for me to be able to do some fieldwork. So I did both; I taught these seminars at Capetown and then went to the bush on that money.

And the irony is, guess who has been complaining to me most recently about not being able to get any money? Raymond Thompson.

Sugar Ray?

Yeah, they treat him the same way for different reasons, but they don't give him any money either. It's the little bullshit, hot flush proposals that are out there.

I thought they were giving money to the big names.

Oh, that's [not] happened recently. There is money going allocationally, that is, indirectly, to big names. That is, there's a kind of belief now that if you are working on the, say, very early time ranges like [Glynn L.] Isaac, digging the sites like Leakey, that's important. That should be supported regardless of who you are. In a sense, if you consider Glynn Isaac a big name, he is getting money, but because it is considered to be important no matter how it is done to dig up early man. But I would be very surprised—[Richard S.] MacNeish gets turned down regularly.

Do you want to go back in the field?

Yeah, I do.

Do you have something in mind?

Yeah, but I'm going to have to fund it another way. I'll never get money from NSF. I'm going to a private foundation.

2

EXPLAINING THE NEW ARCHAEOLOGY

Who coined the term "New Archaeology"?

Joe Caldwell and Bob Braidwood coined the phrase "New Archaeology." It was a pejorative term when used by Braidwood. It was dubbed the "New Archaeology"—I mean, it was bullshit archaeology, as Braidwood used the term.

[Joe Caldwell first used the term in a positive sense] in an article published in *Science* in the mid- to late fifties [1959]. He was talking about all the new things—the new hardware, C-14, attribute, and all the various approaches. And when we began to talk about inferring social organization and all these things, people thought of this as an extension of the New Archaeology as defined by Caldwell. It was just what [was] new.

But he was talking about technique while you were moving into methodology.

We were moving into methodology and theory. There came a point at which, when we began really to in a sense attack or argue against established people like Braidwood. Braidwood took this condescending view, "Now young man, when you grow up, you will see with an older and wiser head." He used the term "New Archaeology" sort of like "kiddie archaeology." Instead of arguing against it, we said, "Okay, if that's what you want to call us, that's fine." But Braidwood really was the one who made the kind of self-consciousness that was needed to say, "Okay, we are New Archaeologists. We're going to do it; we'll show you." Because up until that time most of us had been just trying to do things newer and better and realizing that new must somehow—at least have the potential to [accomplish] new things. It then became a sociological phenomenon. It was no longer just a continuation of what everybody else was trying to do.

Who was part of it?

At that time it was largely [Kent] Flannery, me, Sally [Binford], Stuart Struever, Bill Longacre, Les Freeman, Bob Whallon, and Chris Peebles; that was the group at Chicago, that we began to think of ourselves as a sociological phenomenon, that we are somehow different from them.

Why did you say that the "New Archaeology" is optimistic?

Any time you are in the pursuit of knowledge, it's optimistic. Any time you say, "We have all the knowledge we need," it is pessimistic. It is not necessarily pessimistic to say, "There's a lot of things I do not know." It's only pessimistic to say we cannot know them. If you look at what was going on in archaeology in the '50s, you had people like [Christopher] Hawkes and [Robert] Wauchope and lots of people saying, "There are some things we *cannot* know because of the limitations of the archaeological record, and it is foolish to even try." This was largely in response to [Walter] Taylor, who was saying we should know more things. The negative response to Taylor was to say, "That is inappropriate even to think." So there was this pessimistic side to archaeology in response to Walt Taylor, and a lot of people standing and saying, "We can't even know—I just want to know what the pottery type is or what the date is." Or, "We can only describe the archaeological record. We can only tell you what [we've] found; we cannot tell you what all those things like social organization and all is about because that's beyond. . . . We can only tell you the facts." Strict empiricist position.

I saw that as pessimistic, you see. And there were even those who would say that inference is bad because you can only talk about the facts. If you make an inference from the facts, then you've gone away from the empirical world. Inference is bad. I had been trained the Boasian way. I kind of felt uneasy with the idea of inference. [Then] I realized that that was nonsense—every statement that everybody was making about the past was in fact an inference. No matter how guarded and conservative it was, it was still an inference. So the question was not whether or not to make inferences; the question was how you justify and prove them. So the whole testing and justification thing was what was important, not whether or not you make [inferences]. Everybody was making them.

What are you inferring from the data?

How it came into being, most of the time. What are the conditions in the past that brought into being what you see today? That's what you are inferring—the past. You are inferring anything that you say about the past—social structure, et cetera. You want to be able to justify your inferences. Proof is a hard master, because [it is impossible to] say that you ever know anything absolutely. But one can argue; one can be greatly concerned with the way one justifies an inference. And it's in recognizing the limitations of this that you admit that you are actively in the pursuit of knowledge. And you can only be then if you admit that there is something you don't know. In the past the archaeologists were perfectly willing to say, "We don't know what is found in central Kansas." But none of them would say, "We don't know how to interpret what we find after we find it." I was saying, "Knowing what's in central Kansas is a contemporary phenomenon. Knowing what it means is where we have to admit our ignorance and be concerned with how do you justify or evaluate the way in which you give meaning to what you see." So most traditional archaeologists would be asked, "You think you know everything?" [They would] say, "Heavens, no. I don't know what's in such and such a site down on the Illinois River; I wish I could dig it." If you were to ask me, "What is it you don't know?" I'd say, "I don't know what the meaning of this pattern is; I don't know what high frequency of bones versus a low frequency of tools means; I don't know what the archaeological record means." And that is the challenge—being able to give meaning to it accurately and being able, in turn, to recognize where your ignorance [is] and where your strength is. You can only really build an argument from knowledge. So you have to know what is secure knowledge in order to move against your ignorance.

You are still saying that there is
no secure knowledge from the archaeological record?

That's right. No science ever says that. That's back to where we really started: every time you learn something new, it impacts on everything you ever thought you knew in some sense. So it is a continuous pursuit.

When can you get down to making laws?

Laws are just a series of statements about the constraints on your knowledge. You can do that at any point. A law can be wrong. A law is a statement about the way the world works—about the causal mechanisms of the world. Nobody can see cause. I have lawlike statements about the way the world works. I must deduce the consequences of those beliefs for experience. And that's a hypothesis. A hypothesis is what I expect the world to be like if my ideas of how it works are correct. So hypotheses are derived from theories. They are not statements of theory that you then try to go out and verify.

Theories are not verifiable directly, because you can never see cause directly. This is old [David] Hume's problem—with the billiard balls. We've known that for a long time. You can't see cause directly. All you see is symptomatic properties of cause because cause is something we invent to explain the world. It is an invention of ours.

Where do your assumptions come from?

Assumptions are important in theory building and in the statement of laws, and in specifying the conditions under which you say, "Okay, maybe it doesn't work this way everywhere, but under these conditions it always works this way." So how do you specify the conditions for your theories? All of those are part of your theory and condition how you can deduce and test a hypothesis. I've written about the Bordes thing; that is a chapter in *In Pursuit of the Past*, the Thames and Hudson book.

How do you characterize New Archaeology today in contrast to how you were teaching it in the early '60s?

In the early '60s, basically it was a negative teaching strategy. That is, it was [to] take a given field report and say this is not being done right for the following reasons, and to try and then explore with the students other ways of doing things, but at the technical level. So I taught courses like statistics and mathematics in the early '60s. I don't teach that anymore at all. I taught surveying courses and mapping and field techniques courses in the '60s—lots of stuff like that—whereas now I'm teaching more courses in theory building and how to think and philosophy—that sort of stuff.

Also, in the '60s, I think I taught more case study–type courses. That is, I would take a student, and he would be digging a site here or there. We would take the data from his little site and try and figure out what you can do with [them] to get more information out about the past. My approaches now are much more global and comparative than that. If I have a student now who's got a site, what I try to do is get him to read everything there is known about hunters and gatherers or horticulturalists or whatever in order to be able to put that site in some kind of perspective—not be so introspective about it. That's a big change in the way I teach. Basically, we'd take a site and then we'd try to milk it to death. And half of it would be sheer speculation, which was okay with me because the speculation—as long as it was plausible—proved that the methods of traditional archaeology would never have gotten there. [Let's say] I can take a body of data and weave a plausible argument—that is, if this had happened in the past, it would account for what we saw. Then I could immediately turn and show you that the methods of traditional archaeology would never admit that as a plausible conclusion, okay? So that in a sense shows the limitations of the old method, but it didn't have a method to get there, just beyond sheer force of imagination.

In terms of method, are you talking at all about systems analysis?
Not in the systems sense, no. When I said I was talking about systems, I meant that in the most general sense of the word. We were dealing with the by-products of organizations; and an organization is a set of self-interacting relationships among a series of parts; and the archaeological record is a manifestation of this. I may have a part here and a part there and a part somewhere else, and the challenge is to [know] how they related together in the active phase in the past. . . . [T]raditional archaeology made the assumption that a cultural system is an internally homogeneous phenomenon. What you see archaeologically—any site is as good as any other site for manifesting the norms

and values of the people who participated in the culture. So when I talked about systems I was talking about a totally different paradigmatic expectation about the world. Traditional archaeologists thought that the archaeological record was a manifestation of persons' ideas and values and that a culture was [a system] that had an internally homogeneous set of values so that the criterion of similarity allows you to identify cultures. I was saying a cultural system [is] internally differentiated. It's made up of different parts organized and formed differently. So that I can have a site over here and a site over there that are totally different. The criterion of similarity would never allow you to group them as similar cultures, yet they would simply be parts of a cultural system.

Give an example.

Well, you have them in your house. If I dug up your kitchen versus your bedroom, and I didn't know they went together, they have totally different content and so they would be in different cultures, in the traditional sense of the word.

What do you teach students today about your philosophy of science?

Mary Ann [Binford's wife at the time of the interview] and I were talking about that last night. Children—one of the most frightening things that a child can experience is to think that he's totally unique and therefore totally alone. This is true of a student as well. And if you were telling a student, "You're being trained to think, to use to the best advantage your own thoughts," and that student doesn't know anything about the thoughts that have been made by people accepting similar challenges in the past, he immediately feels alone.

I was never too short of self-confidence as a student. But it's a big thing to sit in a field surrounded by all the symbols of academic excellence and to say, "I trust my thoughts more than

I trust the thoughts of the authorities in the field." That's a hell of a thing to finally decide you're going to do. In public I presented this confident image, but in private, quiet, it's a very frightening thing because you're literally saying—I'm saying that my thoughts are valuable, and they're more valuable than his and his and his. Now how do I not just *assert* that they are valuable but how do I *demonstrate* their value?

Now it may be very simple. It may be that [my idea is] not a new idea at all, and Aristotle already said it better five different ways, and I'm a dumbbell sittin' there and makin' a fool out of myself. That's quite a possibility. So if I don't know what all the rest thought, the men who really invested in thinking, I could make a total fool out of myself. So one of the prerequisites is to say, To what degree is the thinking I'm having in any way new? Or, even more important, it may not be new but it may be addressing a new problem. Thoughts themselves are new not by virtue of my innovation but by my taking the raw material of past thinkers to a new situation.

If I know what I'm doing, then I can say with confidence what I'm thinking. And that's basic to being a student, I think. If I don't know what other people have thought and know what they [did, I cannot contribute to the] intellectual culture. Because if you can't, you then are like a kid, you know. I mean, maybe I'm really being dumb when I think I'm smart.

Unless no one around you knows that stuff either.

That's right.

That's what's so scary about students.

Sure. Or they will rediscover the wheel on a daily basis and not know it. Mary Ann is in a meeting today and all this week. There's all this money available for trying to talk about what demands the school system will have to meet in the future. And there's all of this push to train the kids to do computers and all that; and I said, bullshit—they'll have to learn that on their own. What they have to learn is how to place themselves in some kind of perspective. You have to have a basic liberal education. If you go in the direction of more and more technical training, you've just blown our society.

I would modify what you say, because if you do not get the girls on the machines, they're going to have computer fear just like my generation had math anxiety. But that should be a small part of the education.

Well, I'm not saying they shouldn't use the current technology, but I'm saying the thrust of trying to mold a more and more technically oriented educational system is backwards.

Back to philosophy of science. You were saying there is no absolute knowledge when the tape recorder went off.

Right. At any one point in time you could say absolutely that this is what we know, but you can't say absolutely that that's all there is to know, or that that's adequate if other knowledge changes. So all you can do is assess the knowledge tools that you have available at any one point in time and then figure how to use them to address ignorance. We're not trying to create absolute truths. That's the difference between science and a religion.

A religion is trying to say what the bottom line is, which is going to be for now and always has been, and what people are like, and what gods are like, and what morals are like, and all these things. And they're immutable; they're absolutes. Science is literally trying to assess the state of the art of our ability to use the knowledge that we have available to us at any one point in time. Western religions—not all religions but many Western religions—are literally saying that man shouldn't use his ability of rational thought to understand the world because that is in a sense an uppity position. Real understanding comes from accepting truth from authority, the ultimate authority being God, who has given it down in the Bible, or whatever. The powers of reasoning that we have are just watered down versions of the godly ability, and we should never try to usurp those arguments from authority with our own poor little wisdom.

A science is saying, I don't know about absolutes; I don't know about authorities; I never met God; I don't know whether the Bible's true. I am trying to perfect my skills as a rational being, and the skills I'm able to mount at any one point in time are a function of my progress. It is not a function of my capturing an absolute because I—at that point—am denying there is one. I'm just saying that there's varying degrees of my ignorance and my knowledge and they're mixed up together.

3

ANTECEDENTS: EARLY INFLUENCES

Let's talk about your family background.

My father was from the Appalachian hill country; my mother was from the Tidewater area of Virginia. They were from very different kinds of social backgrounds. And in a sense the culture that I was getting from my mother was this elitist [view that] only appears in certain parts of this country. The elitist notion that family background, worth and value, who's good and who's bad, and all the prejudice that you could imagine were there. And my father's philosophy was a little different than that. He was, for the time, a very liberal person, socially and otherwise. And all this difference was played out in the context of the crash of '29. My family had been . . . a number of parts of my family really suffered. They were urban people who were blown away by the depression. So when I was beginning to remember things, it was this ludicrous situation. . . .

My mother's home in Virginia was a very nice, big, old house. But the living room was partitioned off into two bedrooms; the dining room was partitioned off into another little sitting room and a bedroom. Every part of the house was recycled for accommodating all the family members who were out of work. So, a house that was designed for one family, or an extended family—there were three to four nuclear families living in it at one time.

Only one person working—my father; only one person taking care of the house—my grandmother; and all these people sitting around saying how horrible the world is and letting other people wait on them.

At the same time—at this point I had lots of uncles, and laps to sit in, and they were telling me how important and wonderful the family is, when none of them had any money, none of them had anything to eat, and nothing but pretensions. In other words, the situation that I can remember most was one in which what I was being taught had absolutely no relationship to the reality I was experiencing. And there was no way a little kid [could] resolve this other than just be blown away by the whole thing. They're the first memories I have of seeing the world as totally hypocritical.

Did you talk with your father about this?

Yeah. My father was very important in my life. And eventually he got me out of the whole scene on my mother's side of the family.

This business of testing, taking the ideas that you are given and taking them to experience as a test of their utility—that was the way I grew up: that all of these ideas were crap by virtue of the experiences laid right out in front of me. So I guess that was something I was ready for when I began to learn it in college, or high school—what science is all about: using experience to evaluate the idea.

He must have been supporting all these people.

Yeah, he was. He was a very kind man; he never really criticized these people about the fact that they couldn't find a job or wouldn't try to find one. His attitude was, literally, consciously, to tell me, "Okay, it's a shame what these people believe, but that is over; the Civil War is over; the society that they have been telling you about has long since been gone; and you're going to have to live in a world that's so different from what they think the world is like, so the challenge is not to learn all that stuff but to try and figure out what the future's going to be." That was his philosophy. So everything he taught us was that we didn't [shouldn't] accept—receive knowledge [from]—the culture that we were being programmed to. Because it wasn't going to be there; it *already* wasn't there. Our job was to find out how to get along in a world that they had never even conceived of yet. My father would say things like that.

Did your father still have relatives up in the Appalachias? Did you visit?

Oh, we had lots of 'em. Yeah, all the time.

Your mother allowed this?

Yeah. I lived up there several times. There were situations during the '30s where there was not money enough to heat the houses, so the kids would be moved around wherever there was somebody in the general family system that could take care of the kids. In the winter of 1936, nobody had money enough to heat the houses so we were packed off to various places.

Did your Appalachian kin balance your mother's family?

I don't know. It kind of split loyalties. My mother was not well liked by my father's relatives. A lot of them would be very overtly critical to me of my mother. And I guess I felt that was unfair. I didn't like them for that so I didn't know how to respond. What did they want from me? So I tended not to be as warm to them frequently as maybe I would have been had they behaved differently. That was not all of them, but some of them were that way.

My grandmother Binford died when I was about twelve. Incredible lady—really something, just amazing. Her attitude was, "All right, there's no problem that can't be solved if you put your mind to it and you work hard." And the total attitude was a reverse [of that of my mother's kin]. That is, instead of thinking there are some things that are too menial, that are below me, there was nothing too menial for my grandmother. In other words, if that was what was needed, that's what she would do, and she'd do it best that anybody had ever done it. That was her attitude.

She was a mountain woman who wore a sunbonnet and big skirts, and she kept animals—I thought she knew everything about everything in the whole world. She knew all about animals; she knew all about hunting; she knew how to cook; she knew how to plant; she knew how to grow crops; she knew how to do everything, as far as I was concerned. So she was about as different a model as I got in my mother's family as you could imagine. She was the model of what I thought I'd like to be like.

Did she apply it to you?

Oh yeah, she would sit down and tell me what I should do and what I shouldn't do and what I should listen to and what I shouldn't. She was an atheist. She took a dim view of what she called that city-folk stuff. She was quite a character.

Where was your paternal grandfather?

He had died when my father was young. My father had reared that family before he had his own. He had taken care of them. He was the oldest and had worked to take care of his brothers and sisters after his father had died. My father was quite a bit older than my mother.

My mother went up on a trip into the mountains and met him on a romantic weekend. They were married less than four months after they met. He didn't come to Virginia right away. He was a labor organizer in the coal mines and also had worked as a mine electrician. And all his brothers and relatives did coal mine work. But he left the mines to work near my mother's family in Virginia.

During the depression my dad was in an accident [at H. J. Heinz Company]. His legs were partly crushed, so he thought he was going to be crippled. He turned out not to be. They thought they were going to have to take his leg off from gangrene at one point. But he was really in bad shape and there was no pension or paying funds or anything like that in those days. If you can't work, that's it. Things were rough.

Once my mother got back in that scene [i.e., returned to her family in Virginia], the expectations there were staggering. There were all these cultural expectations of what a proper southern woman should do and shouldn't do and whether you should ever have dirt on you. God, it was just amazing.

Yet your maternal grandmother was doing it.

She was taking care of the kitchen, but it was this grin-and-bear-it approach. My grandmother was amazing. She did all of this, but, by God, when she came in [the room], you thought the queen had arrived. She dressed for dinner. And we had black servants until way into the '30s.

Were all these people unemployed?

Yup.

How did you manage that?

They got the table scraps. They didn't have a job. They were the same blacks that worked all along. Same ones. They got dinner scraps and had these loyalties to my family. Amazing. I had a black nurse when I was a child, and it was not until the job market opened up that in a sense the black servants disappeared. Because they continued in a role, and they just got clothing, hand-me-downs. They had no security, but they stayed in that [role] during the early part of the depression.

What did your father do in Virginia?

When he first went back to work, he sold peanuts at the baseball games. And then he got a job as a shipping clerk for H. J. Heinz and Company, and ran a warehouse, and did that until he retired.

And that was enough to take care of all of those people?

That's what they did. But he ran the main warehouse for the distributor of H. J. Heinz for the whole area. And that's what he did the rest of his life.

What about you?

My father was always trying to get me out of my grandparents' house. Sometimes he took me to his family in Appalachia. From eleven on, I lived on and off at home. Sometimes I lived with cousins; sometimes I lived with Dad in an apartment on the harbor in Norfolk [Virginia]. Dad believed in pushing me out in the world. I once had a job—this is the honest truth—sweeping up the only strip joint in Norfolk. Cleaning it out and taking care of backstage. We were living in a little apartment on the harbor in Norfolk, and this burlesque place was right on the harbor near where we lived. My father heard that there was a job there and he . . . I suspect he checked it out to see if I was going get hurt or anything. Because before that I was loading coal into apartment burners. It was really hard work and I was tired all the time in school. He didn't like that. He didn't want me to work so hard.

By that time I had learned of an old retired ship captain named Mr. Holland. I spent lots of time with him, sat on the wharf and listened to stories. A wonderful old man. Dad thought this was a good place—it was all right—but I shouldn't be tired all the time. I fell asleep all the time in school. So he arranged for me to sweep out the burlesque house. I was a kid, but I'd work evenings and clean up the dressing rooms and stuff like that. I was about twelve. And every famous stripper there was of that era I saw and knew and she would pat me on the head.

I guess you didn't have to worry about drugs so much in those days.
Oh, no. Drugs were there. I smoked marijuana when I played in a black band for a while—the trumpet. But the men who ran the places, they were interesting people. Most of them were retired from the navy or merchant marine, and they just had a total view of the world that was so different from my mother's family as to what life should be, what you should live for. They all thought that life really should be travel. Almost all of them, including Mr. Holland. What you should live for is to be able to move. It was sort of their philosophy. If you're in one place too long, then you're a failure.

•

What were some of the other jobs you were doing as a kid?
Well, mainly I was in construction work. That's where I learned it. I worked all through high school in construction work. And my first wife was my boss's daughter. The man I worked for was A. C. Mock and my first wife was Jean Mock. I started working as a common laborer digging ditches; then he moved me into apprenticing in various ways. Then when the union came into Virginia, I was given a master mason's rating on a grandfather clause, and I was sixteen. A grandfather clause means that you've been doing the work of a master mason before the union arrived so you don't have to go through an apprenticeship. And I worked construction work a long time later. For instance, when I got married I worked for A. C. in the interim between this and that—between the army and the new school [the University of North Carolina].

And when I went away to college in anthropology at UNC, I started my own little business. I had my own little construction business in Chapel Hill, and we built houses and whatnot, using veterans that were living in veterans' housing as my crew. Every Saturday I had a lineup for payday outside my apartment in veterans' housing, paying the people who were working for me.

You say that you formed your own company in Chapel Hill?

I really knew a lot about construction from all the years working for A. C., who was a contractor. I just took the exams and passed them.

Which gave you the right to be a general contractor?

Yeah. You see, in veterans' housing at North Carolina in those days, it was packed with people who had incredible skills. And we all lived in these old army barracks at Chapel Hill. And I knew almost everybody on my block, so we'd sit around saying, How can we make money? I had the contractor's license. And we started doing land surveys because the only equipment you need for that is a transit, and [we could] borrow that from the school.

So we used to check out transits from the engineering department and go out and do land surveys with them. What happened was interesting because once I started doing land surveys, most of these were in the context of somebody selling or buying farmland. Almost inevitably, either one [buyer] or the other [seller], somebody would say, "Do you know anybody who could fix that barn over there?" Because this is the time when repair is always done, right? When ownership changes.

It became clear that I had all kinds of opportunities to do repair work; so then I started doing short-term, small repair jobs and hiring people. But that is the riskiest business in construction work, and I knew that, because once you give somebody an estimate on repairing something and then you tear the building down and find out that what you thought was solid wood was rotten, it's a bummer.

So the next thing I did, there was a law passed in North Carolina that said that businesses and so forth couldn't set their garbage out on the street uncovered because it attracted flies. So all the fraternity houses on campus had to construct these little garbage houses. So I said, "Aha, we'll bid on all the garbage houses. And we've got a good chance because we're members and veterans and we're part of the university." So we went to the interfraternity council on campus and made a blanket bid to build all their garbage houses. And we got the contract. And we made enough off of that to buy a truck and a mortar mixer and some other pieces of equipment. And then we started building houses in town.

What was your religious training?

Intense [big laugh]. My parents—my mother's family had been Methodists. And they really believed. I've been reared in that. (My father was a Baptist, but he went to Methodist church with my mother.) Well, the first kind of rebellion was correlated with the family situation. But part of the pulling out of my mother's family involved my friend Harry Bowen. I began this strategy of saying I want to go to another church—not the church where my mother went—because I wanted to be with my friend Harry. And Mother said that was all right. So I went to the Episcopalian church with Harry, and that's where I met my first girlfriend. The girl didn't last very long, but I realized I was going to church and I wasn't under the constraints of my parents. So then I became Episcopal. And I went through this whole thing. I converted and went through all the training that you have to do, and I actually joined the Episcopal church. So this was then a legitimate way of no longer going to church with my parents.

Did you believe it?

Yeah. I believed most of it. They believed us. At that point I hadn't come to the point of questioning the religion thing, just the social components of it. And the real questioning about religion as such grew out of the social scene in the South in those days because I guess I had from very early on been attuned to spying hypocrisy, and you would hear all this argument about man and God and all these things, and so the situation with the blacks was something that seemed to me to be totally at odds with what you heard. So, why aren't the blacks in this church? Because they're different. Why? And so, it was really the social hypocrisy of the South that made me question religion because it was always . . . the justification for everything was always back in the religious camp. This is the way God meant it to be, blah, blah. And then here was this situation that was totally inconsistent with what I was hearing. Nobody talked about it.

I guess it was working with blacks; I worked a lot with blacks on construction crews. In fact, most of the time I was the only white on the labor gangs. And later I played in a black band. When I began to hear these people's attitudes about white culture, then the hypocrisy was clear. But it was not until that happened that I was working construction with lots of blacks and in many cases I would be the only white on the crew, mainly because I was so young, so that you were either black or a child, which qualified you to dig ditches. And it was from working with black labor gangs that I began to be less than happy with all the church nonsense.

Why didn't you go into your father's branch of the religion?

Basically, I thought that was worse because most of the shoutin' Baptists didn't amount in this world. They were less liberal than Methodist preachers were.

Who do you feel was influential in your life?

My father, obviously. And the very setting of my mother's family provided the framework in which I saw things, was forced to view things. I didn't have to like all the things for them to be influential.

Another thing, perhaps surprising, is that once we had in a sense gotten out of the family situation, the thing that I really began investing in. . . . Public school didn't ever [engage me] except for a very few courses that turned me on. I avoided public school. I didn't go very often because we were working and you could always claim in those days that working was more important than going to school. And I always had something I was doing. So I really didn't go to school very much.

But what I really did invest in was the Boy Scouts. They were extremely important to me in those days. For me personally, this was a place where all the emphasis was on learning; it was not on form. In school, the emphasis was on form, on speaking the English language properly. That's what I heard from my mother's family: sitting up properly, doing table manners properly. The emphasis was on the cultural side, the proper side. This was what I got out of school, you know, how to do the multiplication tables properly—you're supposed to learn them in sequence. You can't just know how to multiply; you have to be able to recite the multiplication tables.

Do you think that's wrong?

Absolutely.

Why?

Because that's not the way I learned to multiply. It has nothing to do with multiplication being able to [work for you]. . . . It's like the ABC's—why does anybody want to recite the ABC's? Nobody uses them that way. Why should I have to recite them? That was the emphasis at school—on the form. And not on learning, not on the role that it plays in giving you raw material to work with in terms of thinking but on the form of it all. So I rejected it. I just didn't like that. But in the Scouts, that was not the emphasis. The leaders that I had could care less about how you did something. They were interested in creating more and different kinds of experiences for you to in a sense take out what turns you on and then invest in it yourself. So that was really . . . I learned all kinds of things in the Scouts, . . . mainly in the whole area of understanding nature. We worked in swamps and studied everything we could possibly study.

Was that the influence that got you interested in biology?

Yeah, sure. And it actually started me having a peripheral interest in archaeology. There was all this romantic notion about Indians, you know, and their relation to the environment. And we used to go out and find sites and pick up arrowheads if we could find them. The first pieces of actual work I did in archaeology were on places that I had learned about through the Scouts. My thesis was on an area in Virginia, and almost all of those sites and the people—landowners, et cetera—were people that I had gotten to know during the war, between 1943 and 1945, when I was in the Scouts.

What were you interested in as a kid?

Animals, snakes, owls; knowing all the trees and why they were different; and just being able to anticipate natural events—knowing when the ducks would come in on the marshes. I got tremendous satisfaction out of being able to predict natural events, about seasonality.

What made you want to do that?

It seemed to be something that one could learn about without having to go through all these forms, conventions—how to sit up straight and hold your knife. It was as far away from the social nonsense that characterized a lot of my life as you could get. Ducks didn't talk back.

Did you have a dog?

Yeah, I did. I had a dog named Trixie, a spitz, a really neat dog, for fourteen years. Her hair fell out half the time. She had raw back sores. A neat, neat dog, though.

Do you keep contact with anyone back there?

Umhmm. There was a fellow that I went through school with by the name of Henry Bernick. He still lives in Norfolk and works for the Norfolk public school system, and he's in charge of the music program for the entire school system. And Henry and I were great friends as children. We keep in touch.

And there's an English teacher that I had that I've kept in touch with. She was really neat because all up until I had her, I had always failed English. I told her I couldn't write. I don't know why but she kind of thought I was fun, I guess, or a challenge perhaps. When I went to her class, I'd learned from all these other teachers in junior high that I didn't know English right. So I told her, one day when I saw her. She was walking down the steps one day when the school was closing; I saw her and said, "I haven't known you before, but I guess I owe you to tell you that I'm not very good in English."

She said, "Where'd you get such an idea?"

I said, "Well, that's what the teachers have always told me." She says, "Well, we'll change that."

And I couldn't believe it. She says, "I want you to come and see me this week." Really interesting woman. I went to see her. She says, "I don't believe what you just told me. I don't believe you are dumb in English. And if I can do something, will you change the way you think about yourself?"

I said, "What do you mean?"

She says, "You know, there's a state poetry contest in which they [give an] award at the state level every year to the high school student who writes the most original poem. If you can win the state contest, will you change the way you think about yourself?"

I said, "You've got to be crazy. I *hate* poetry." And before the year was out, I entered the state poetry contest and won something.

Do you still have the poem?

Oh, yeah.

One stormy morn', I chanced to meet a lassie in the town.
Her locks were like the ripening wheat;
Her laughing eyes were brown.
I watched her as she tripped along, 'til madness filled my brain,
And then and then I know 'twas wrong, I kissed her in the rain.

With raindrops shining on her cheek like dewdrops on a rose,
The little lassie strove to speak my boldness to oppose.
Then standing there and quivering, her fingers stole in mine;
Then the birds began to sing, and the sun began to shine.

And I am proud as any prince; all honors I disdain.
She says I am her rain-beau since I kissed her in the rain.

That's marvelous. How did your teacher get you from nothing to that?

She just kept telling me, "Look, don't you talk? Don't you talk to your friends? Don't you think it's fun? Well, let's make it more fun. See what you can do. What are the limits of its use?" A super teacher.

But you still have a reputation as being rough around the edges in language.

Sure.

How do you feel about that, then?

I think they're fools [much laughter].

Okay, you believe her evaluation of your writing, and you still correspond with her?

Yeah. Her name was Mrs. Henning. You see, once again this is the form business. If I'm trying to say something that I don't think has been said, there's no trite way of saying it. A cliché is usually pretty meaningless and also obvious to anyone who reads it. If you're trying to say something with the same words that everybody else is using, but you think you don't want them to think about it the same way, you have to play with the way you use words. If an editor or person reads my sentence, which I wrote in clear prose, and says, "Yeah, I know what you're saying," then I know that he missed the point; and I take that sentence and make a whole paragraph out of it to make sure that he understands what is different about what I am saying. I write so that people have got to read and reread it so that maybe they have got the meaning.

Why? Why didn't you think the first time worked?

Because they translated it into what they *thought* I was saying, not what I *was* saying. In a sense, the clearer writing is, the more ambiguous the terms are. . . . In other words, the clearest sentence would be the sentence that everybody would give meaning to immediately. But the degree [to which] they all do it the same way is not at all clear.

You mean in scientific writing.

That's right. And if I'm trying to manipulate a reader, I can't do it by making him think he knows what I'm saying. Because if I think I'm saying something that he doesn't know, or I think I'm saying something new, then why should he think it's all so clear and he's thought it all along?

Good point. Here you are living with your father, and you went through high school. Were you doing sports in high school?

Uh-huh. I did normal things. I played basketball, football, baseball.

Tell me about your college and military years.

I finished high school in January of 1948 and started college the following September. I went to VPI in 1948. VPI was a B.A. program. I had a little bit of money to start college. I went to college on an athletic scholarship—for football at VPI. I quit after a while. I was exhausted, and I got turned on to the classes. I thought the classes were incredible; I was blown away. I hadn't expected that. And I found trying to play football, and eat at the training table (which was late meals)—and we practiced all afternoon and had all our classes in the morning. We'd start practice at noon or 1:00; we'd go through 'til supper; we'd eat on the training table; we'd get back to the room at 7:30 at night, and then I was supposed to do homework? It just didn't work.

So I resigned, and the counselor said, "Well, now, don't resign. Wouldn't you like to play lacrosse? The practice is not as long; the season is short." So I said okay, and I tried it. But that was worse because I didn't know how to do that. And practice was in many ways rougher. Lacrosse in those days—oh, my God—we'd hit each other on the head with a wooden stick. So I just then dropped the whole athletic program and I worked literally as a cowboy.

VPI was an ag[ricultural] school and they had all these experimental herds of cattle, which they used in the agricultural school for feed tests and seeing how cattle would respond to this and that. And so every day I'd go down to the barn and they'd give me a list—the cattle all had ear tags with numbers—a list of the cows from the herd they wanted brought into the barns to be experimentally fed or . . . I'd take a little cutting horse named

Pencil. I'd go down and cut the cattle out of the herd and drive them down to the barns and check 'em in. That's what I'd do every afternoon. That's how I paid for my room and board, working at the cow barn.

You lived at the college?

Oh, yeah. [One day] I was sitting around trying to figure out how to get money to [complete] college. I had already given up athletics at that point, because I could not do both. . . . So in my junior year I just said, "Okay, we'll take a chance," because they were then offering the GI Bill again for Korean service. So I enlisted simply to get the GI Bill again so that I could go back to finish college. I was in the army from late 1951 or 1952 to the beginning of 1954. This was right after I married Jean Mock, A. C. Mock's daughter.

What did you do in the army?

I went in during the Korean War but never saw action. During basic training, I was sent to leadership school. While waiting for my orders, I was sent to Indian Gap, Pennsylvania, where I trained recruits. That is where our son, Clinton, was born. I continued to take courses through the extension program but did not complete the degree at VPI.

What was your rank in the army?

A corporal. I went to officers' training school because I was encouraged to do so. That was traumatic. I was really uptight about that because by this time I was having real trouble with military philosophy. And I nearly finished officers' candidate school [OCS] training at Fort Benning [Georgia]; I was being set up to take troops to Korea and take them right into combat. And I didn't mind going to combat—I was not trying to get out of combat. What I minded was, I was very upset about trying to propagandize the troops. The leadership role that we were being taught was quite candidly that you're bullshitting these men. These men—nobody cares about these men. They're there on the chess game, and we know we are going to lose 35 percent in this kind of operation and 65 percent in that kind of operation, and yet your job is to make each man think he is going to live when you know his chances are [small]. . . . I really was not happy with that. That was the hypocrisy again. And so I did not finish Officers' Candidate School, thereby refusing the commission at Fort Benning, and went back overseas then as a corporal. And I stayed a corporal. I was discharged as a corporal.

How did they know to test you?

That was part of OCS. See, when you come out there, you go through a whole testing program in order to get in or to get out. It's interesting. There are regular pipelines in the army. Say you're enlisted and you go right into basic training; then at that juncture, the decision is made as to where you go. It is very quick.

But if you go into a program like I did at OCS and then don't jump into the pipeline—don't take the commission—I was in a holding company. There's no regular role for how do you cope with it. So, literally, what they did was give us tests—endlessly—while we were in that holding company to find out how they were going to assign us because technically in a sense we were overqualified.

It was not just me; there were others who had done the same thing. A whole group refused their [commission]. They had gone all the way through jump school. They were paratroopers and then refused it once they realized what it was all about. And so in my barracks, there was a whole series of men. Most of these guys were extremely intelligent. It was amazing. And so we were overqualified for normal jobs; so they tried to put us in a position [where] we wouldn't be troublemakers. . . . I was assigned this very special job, probably because of that.

I didn't know you were allowed to refuse a commission.

You cannot refuse orders, but you can refuse honors or promotions or anything. You can't refuse orders, though. But when you go into one of these schools, the agreement is that they have the right to wash you out and you have the right to resign from the school, the program—not from the army.

I started out with a military job assignment as a draftsman. For some reason I was given a series of aptitude tests. The military decided that I had great skills in language. Well, I thought this was the silliest thing in the world because I had taken seven years of Spanish and could not speak a word and hated it in high school. The military is all of a sudden telling me that I had aptitude in language. Well, I took it as further proof of the stupidity of the military.

But anyway, they carted me off to military language school where I entered a military program in Japanese. I was sent overseas with an MOS [military occupational specialty] as an interpreter in Japanese and was assigned to the headquarters company for dealing with the local people—as the military would call it, "indigenous personnel." In the meantime, there was a civilian outfit that had been formed to advise the government in dealing with the Japanese population dependent personnel. There was a man named Allen Smith who ran a group including Wayne Suttles, Bill Lebra, and another man by the name of Hall. They made up a group of four. They were supposed to be researching the southern Japanese islands and the Ryukyu Islands to advise the military occupation forces on how to deal with these people. That was part of their work. And the other work was literally designing communities for resettling displaced persons off of Iwo Jima, Saipan, and people whose villages had been blown up. That was how I got to know anything about anthropology, working for them. I got fascinated with the whole thing at that point.

After they left, I was the only expert who knew anything about people and culture and whatnot. I was then assigned to the military headquarters as the consultant or advisor on the local culture. In that capacity, I began to do some things. I started an archaeology program, for instance, to salvage the contents of these tombs that had been torn up for military construction. So I really got more and more into reading about anthropology on my own time.

I taught for a while in a military school. I taught political history of Asia and just did all this research on my own. What had happened is that the general decided that all officers who had received a field-grade commission had to have the equivalent of a college education. So all these officers came to the army military for training. Any of us who had ever had any college education were put in teaching these courses. So I was teaching generals and colonels and everyone Oriental political history. I could teach anything I wanted, so I was interested in actual history, not so much political. I just did infinite reading on Asia and everything and taught the courses at that point.

When I came back I had all this experience in working with a different culture. For instance, when the Japanese peace treaty was signed, they had to collect all the money that the American occupation forces had issued and exchange it for Japanese yen, because now the area was going back to Japanese control. So I was sent literally to walk from one village to another, and I had a Japanese counterpart—we were a team. I was there to talk all these people out of their money, and he was there to give them Japanese yen.

On islands like the Amami-O-shima, Tokuno[-shima]—these places that had never been invaded—these are just neolithic communities with no ties to major political systems beyond their little island. And you just go from one island to another and go through all the ritual and all the hospitality and finally tell these people, "Well, I want your money and he wants to give you more." It was quite an experience. I was insatiably fascinated by the different cultures, which I had never really seen before outside of this country. And I saw everything that came along; I really pushed to see more. I was continually being surprised because I was totally naive [as] to what cultural variability really was. I was continually being surprised: How could these people believe this kind of stuff? I was comparing my own culture to what I was seeing.

The ritual was hospitality. We would go into the headman's house, and we would have a meal. People would come and dance and show things. Most of these people had never seen a Caucasian before. I was their first. They would bring people from the hinterlands to show the kids this strange being.

They weren't literate then?

To some extent. You would have literate persons, but this was historical literacy, not current events literacy. They maybe had read, or could read, or even wrote family lineages, for instance, but there were no newspapers that these people ever read. Not all these islands were even aware of the war. They were not aware either that they were under American control or Japanese control on some of the small islands. They were not quite comfortable with either idea. They thought that they ruled.

How did Jean feel when you went into anthropology?

She was instrumental really in getting me in the state of mind to do so. When I came back from the army, I assumed that I had to work for A. C. for a while doing construction work and eventually would go back to school and maybe follow this dream of forestry or whatever. And . . . but I guess it was clear to her that I was all turned on not by forestry, not by buildings, but by what I had done in the army. And so when I had worked for her father for a while and was getting ready to go back to college, and I had just—see, VPI didn't have married student housing; it was a boys' military school. So I wasn't thinking of going back there at all to follow up on anything.

But you had finished.

Yeah, but I had thought I wanted to go and . . . I couldn't get a job in forestry with the degree I had. So I wanted to do some graduate work. I was thinking about this, and she said, "Look, what do you really want to do?"

I said, "What I really want to do is what I was doing in the army. I want to know more about man and all this."

And there was no school in Virginia that taught anthropology. So I went over to William and Mary Extension and talked to an advisor in sociology. And he said, "Well, they have a department at the University of North Carolina, and it's quite likely that you can get some state subsidy because you have to go out of state because the state doesn't have any such department. And we'll investigate that for you."

That turned out not to be the case with the GI Bill, but in any case I went to North Carolina on his advice. And it was Jean who really said, "If that's what you want to do, do it. You're not locked in to either working for my father or following up on forestry. Do what you want." She was very supportive at that time, in that decision. So I went to UNC in the fall of 1954 and transferred as many credits from VPI as possible. Our daughter, Muffy [Martha], was born during those years. I took lots of electives along with my anthropology courses. I got my B.A. at UNC and enrolled in the M.A. program there. But when I was accepted in the University of Michigan graduate program, I moved there and got the M.A. from Michigan.

TOP: *Lew with his parents, J. Lewis Binford and Eoline Roberts Binford, in the backyard of their home on Colonial Avenue in Norfolk, Virginia. (All photos here and on the following page are courtesy of Lewis R. Binford.)*

ABOVE LEFT: *Lew, at age 10 or 11, with a "canteen" made from Uncle Jimmie's whiskey bottle. Off to the Boy Scouts!*

ABOVE RIGHT: *United States Army induction photo, 1952.*

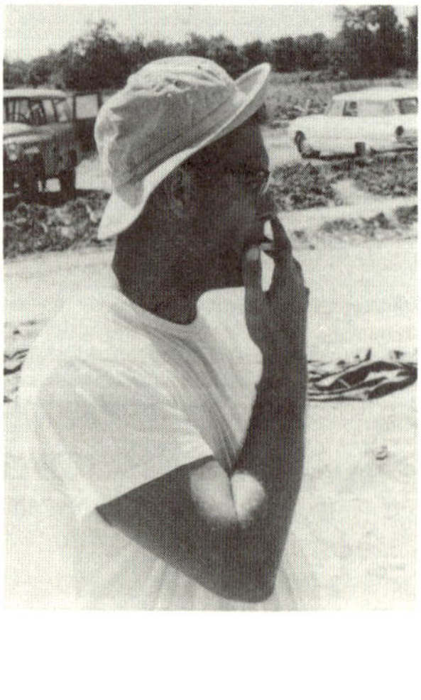

ABOVE: *Archaeological excavation at Roanoke River Basin, North Carolina, 1956. Lew, on the left, was then a student at the University of North Carolina with Stanley South, on the right.*

LEFT: *Lew at the Carlyle Reservation Project, Illinois, 1963. Lew was teaching at the University of Chicago at the time.*

ABOVE: *Looking at Acheulean tools in the Hunsgi Valley with K. Paddayya of Deccan College, June 1986.* Photo courtesy of Nancy Medaris Stone.

RIGHT: *At Southampton University, England, where Lew was awarded the honorary degree of Doctor of Letters in 1980. At the time, he was teaching at the University of New Mexico.* Photo courtesy of Colin Renfrew.

ABOVE: *Lew and wife, Nancy Medaris Stone, 1988.* Photo courtesy of Alexandria King.

BELOW: *Lew and his daughter, Martha Binford, in Terrell, Texas, November 1991.* Photo courtesy of Nancy Medaris Stone.

ABOVE: *Lew with his former University of New Mexico graduate students LuAnn Wandsnider and Robert Hitchcock, on a visit to Lincoln, Nebraska, spring 1992.* Photo courtesy of Nancy Medaris Stone.

RIGHT: *Lew with Luis Borrero at "Luis's Square," the Tunel site, Tierra del Fuego, summer 1994.* Photo courtesy of Nancy Medaris Stone.

POSTSCRIPT

THE INTELLECTUAL LEGACY OF LEWIS R. BINFORD

by Jeremy A. Sabloff

When Lewis Binford launched his professional career at the beginning of the 1960s, the field of American archaeology was like a rudderless ship. While there was growing unhappiness with the status quo, there was no agreement as to how the field might change and where it should head. Although most American archaeologists saw themselves as anthropologists, their intellectual efforts were not generally held in high regard by their anthropological colleagues, and their research was more concerned with recreating culture histories than with building laws of human behavior.

The major achievements in the field in the immediate post–World War II years were in identifying ancient cultures and defining their boundaries through time and space. Thus, by 1960, archaeologists throughout the Americas were constructing increasingly refined cultural sequences in region after region. Previous historical gaps in archaeological understanding were filled in, and knowledge of better-known cultures rapidly expanded. Moreover, a host of scientific tools, particularly C-14 (or radiocarbon) dating, considerably bolstered and strengthened the efforts directed toward chronology building and refinement.

However, if archaeologists at this time were asked how the well-dated cultures functioned, more often than not they could not give many details. Much cultural behavior remained unknown because most of the archaeological cultures were known principally by the types of pottery they made or stone tools they chipped. Although many archaeologists believed that this situation was mainly due to the poverty of the archaeological record, which only preserved limited kinds of nonperishable artifacts, some archaeologists—such as Walter W. Taylor in his volume *A Study of Archaeology*, published in 1948—began to argue that much more information could be squeezed out of the seemingly impoverished archaeological record. Taylor, for example, contended that more attention to the contexts in which artifacts were found could throw more light on the function of the artifacts. In general, some scholars began to argue that the record could be illuminated if only new methods could be devised to accomplish this goal.

The 1950s witnessed the development of one such methodological tool: settlement pattern studies. Settlement research, pioneered by Gordon R. Willey in Peru and subsequently in the Maya area, examines the distributions of cultural activities across landscapes, as in residential areas or manufacturing zones, looking for patterns of cultural-environmental correlation. However, such research did not lead to general explanations and failed to stimulate interest directly in archaeological theory in the 1950s.

By 1958, in a widely read book, *Method and Theory in American Archaeology*, Willey and Philip Phillips reiterated their famous dictum that "archaeology is anthropology or it is nothing." However, they also had to admit that archaeology had accomplished precious little in explaining the processes of culture—that is, the whys and wherefores of cultural change through time—and that relatively few archaeologists evinced any explicit interest in developing theories about such processes.

The Rise of the New Archaeology

Lewis Binford did not believe that the theoretical aspirations of archaeologists had to be limited by the relative poverty of the archaeological record. Picking up on Willey and Phillips's challenge, he felt that archaeologists could contribute to anthropological theory. In 1962, he forcefully expressed this optimistic viewpoint in a landmark article in *American Antiquity*, the flagship journal for American archaeology. In this article, entitled "Archaeology as Anthropology," Binford stressed the anthropological relevance of archaeology. However, in order to achieve such relevance and contribute to the building of theories about the nature of cultural development, Binford argued that archaeologists had to change their ways of examining the archaeological record. He contended that they had to abandon their emphasis on the listing of cultural traits (kinds of pottery, stone tools, and so on) and begin to look at culture as a system. Artifacts should be related to the "structural and functional characteristics of cultural systems" (1962:218), and their roles in the technological, social, and ideological subsystems of culture should be examined. Moreover, archaeologists needed to move beyond description (what Binford termed "explication") and attempt explanation. It was not sufficient, Binford claimed, to muster evidence that a migration occurred; archaeologists should further attempt to explain *why* it occurred. He closed the article by boldly stating: "As archaeologists, with the entire span of culture history as our 'laboratory,' we cannot afford to keep our theoretical heads buried in the sand. We must shoulder our full share of responsibility within anthropology. Such a change could go far in advancing the field of archaeology, specifically, and would certainly advance the general field of anthropology" (1962:224).

Binford followed up the 1962 paper with two other pathbreaking articles in *American Antiquity*: "A Consideration of Archaeological Research Design" in 1964 and "Archaeological Systematics and the Study of Culture Process" in 1965. In these pieces, he developed some critical ideas that he had briefly broached in 1962. He argued that in order for archaeology to enter a more explanatory mode of operation, it had to develop better research designs. The latter had to be more problem-oriented than before. Archaeologists should not excavate a mound simply because it is there or because it is the biggest mound in the neighborhood, but because excavation would provide answers to a previously posed archaeological question. Moreover, archaeologists need to be concerned with scale, Binford insisted, and should generally endeavor to place sites in broader contexts, such as the region.

Binford also was deeply concerned with cultural variability. If scholars were to move away from a "trait list" view of culture—a theoretical position that Binford labeled "normative"—they would have to discard their emphases on uniformity and homogeneity as well. If archaeologists instead adopted a theoretical view that emphasized the systemic nature of culture, then variability and heterogeneity would become the bywords, since artifacts might have variable meanings in technological, social, or ideological contexts. Regional-scale projects would offer better opportunities to comprehend cultural variability, too, than ones that were purely site-oriented. In addition, the highly promising settlement pattern approach, which had just begun to emerge as a productive field methodology, provided an ideal means by which to pursue regional-scale, problem-oriented studies.

The new interest in a systemic view of culture with its attendant emphasis on cultural variability had another highly important implication for archaeological research design. The new perspective meant that archaeologists had to take a major interest in the question of sampling. Such interest further meant that they had to become proficient in statistics.

Under the traditional, normative approach to the archaeological record, which emphasized homogeneity, it did not usually matter where the archaeologist placed a test pit in a site or which sites were excavated in a region. But, as Binford argued, if homogeneity was not assumed, then obtaining an adequate sample loomed large indeed. For example, if sites had different functions or were occupied in different seasons, then a research strategy had to be structured so that the archaeologist had a reasonable chance to sample varied parts of a site or varied kinds of sites.

Binford further pointed out that another implication of the shift in perspective from a normative to a systems view of culture was that the established conceptual inventory had to be changed. Concepts that derived from a static, normative view of culture would be inadequate to develop a dynamic systems perspective, according to Binford. He proposed to review the existing type concepts, for example, and replace them with ones derived from the new theoretical position. Even more general concepts such as "culture" would have to be shifted to more dynamic ones like "interaction sphere," which could better serve a systems approach.

Finally, in a series of publications in the late 1960s and early 1970s, Binford argued that in order to understand the processes of cultural development, archaeologists had to emphasize two key theoretical approaches: cultural evolution and cultural ecology. Actually, *revive* and emphasize would more adequately describe the situation, as both these approaches had been around for some time. The principal champions of these positions were the anthropologists Leslie White and Julian Steward, although their arguments were ignored by a majority of their colleagues in the field.

Binford derived his systems view of culture from White; from both White and Steward came Binford's belief that the interaction between the environment and the technological subsystem of culture was crucial for understanding the evolution of culture. There further was a natural intellectual link between Binford's view of culture as a system (shared by White) and the systemic view of environmental-human interactions (drawn from the work of Steward). Binford also was influenced by White in his contention that cultural evolution was a general process driven by increasingly efficient human capture and use of energy through time.

Although various components of Binford's polemic for changing the nature of the archaeological enterprise did not originate with him and had been discussed in the anthropological literature, even for a number of years, Binford's genius lay in his ability to pull a variety of diverse intellectual strands together in a highly promising synthesis. Moreover, he was able forcefully and persuasively to show how this synthetic position could solve many of the inadequacies in the traditional pursuit of archaeology that a growing number of its practitioners had come to recognize. Furthermore, he convincingly argued that adoption of the new dynamic paradigm would place archaeology in the forefront rather than at the rear of anthropological attempts to explain the processes of cultural development over long periods of time.

In sum, Binford proposed to revolutionize the practice of archaeology. The shift to an archaeology that was focused on providing explanations of cultural processes that would contribute to general anthropological theory, instead of just describing the past, entailed radical changes in archaeological practices. It also called into question traditional archaeological assumptions about the nature of culture and culture change. For example, Binford mocked what he termed the "aquatic" view of cultural spread from a culture center, which saw a "stream" or "flow" of culture traits from the center to the peripheries. Binford remonstrated against such description by insisting that the terminology disguised the archaeologist's lack of understanding of culture process. *How* did various aspects of culture diffuse from site to site, and *why*? he queried. These were the kinds of questions archaeologists needed to ask, he stated. More important, they needed to understand how change developed internally, as well as externally. Only with such shifts in focus and practice could archaeology become a contributor to anthropological theory.

Successes and Failures

Lewis Binford's polemic had both immediate and long-term impacts. A number of younger scholars, Binford's own students at the University of Chicago as well as students in other departments, were rapidly persuaded by Binford's new agenda for the field. The New Archaeologists (as followers of the movement came to be called) were excited by the new vistas for archaeology that were opened up by Binford's arguments and began a variety of small-scale applications of the systemic perspective. In a much broader sense, the writings and research of Binford and his followers triggered a growing sense of optimism in the field.

Such optimism was bolstered by the research of Binford's students, such as William Longacre and James Hill, who argued, on the basis of their studies in the American Southwest, that various aspects of social organization, including residence patterns (which were of great interest to cultural anthropologists and seemingly beyond the reach of archaeologists) could actually be identified in the archaeological record. Other scholars were able to show how attention to variability allowed them to use alternative interpretations to call into question traditional assumptions. For instance, Howard Winters, working in the midwestern United States, provided a strong argument that three sites with varying artifact inventories and in different environmental settings might be seasonal camps of a mobile hunter-gatherer settlement system rather than occupations of separate cultures.

By the early 1970s within a decade or so of the publication of "Archaeology as Anthropology," New Archaeology—or, to my mind the preferable term, processual archaeology—began to have an impact on the entire field of American archaeology and in the Old World as well, even among scholars who did not consider themselves adherents of the new views. This widening influence could be seen in various aspects of the entire archaeological enterprise. For example, problem-oriented research became more frequent, along with justifications for the significance of the research. Binford and others, including Patty Jo Watson, Steven LeBlanc, and Charles Redman, also emphasized the need for explicit disclosure of archaeologists' assumptions and encouraged researchers to challenge these assumptions whenever possible. In general, there was a rising tide of agreement that archaeologists should strive to move beyond description of the past on to the use of such descriptions as the means for explaining the past. As was often stated, the field should not only tackle questions of what, where, and when but those of how and why, too.

Other indications of the growing influence of Binford and his students could be seen in the new awareness of the importance of sampling and the revival of cultural evolutionary thinking. Interestingly, the writings of cultural anthropologists such as White, Steward, Morton Fried, Elman Service, and other scholars [Robert Carneiro] who published on evolutionary topics seemed to attract much more attention by the 1970s among archaeologists than among their colleagues in cultural anthropology.

The rise of the early processual archaeology was not an unbridled success story, however. Some notable intellectual problems also arose. Some scholars were estranged from the new movement by its strong, argumentative rhetoric. Other potential allies were put off by the occasional harshness of the polemic and the criticisms of traditional archaeology and archaeologists. But more significantly, some archaeologists, who may have been sympathetic to Binford's general aims in the beginning, grew disappointed with the gap between what processual archaeology was promising in the way of revolutionizing the field and what it had produced in the short run. In effect, Binford and his followers fell victim to their own initial rhetorical claims, particularly those that predicted the discovery of general laws of cultural processes. By the early 1970s they had yet to find any significant ones.

After the early criticisms of the anthropological relevance of traditional archaeology, the New Archaeology seemed to lose headway. Much of its attention and energy appeared to be routed toward examples that showed how the archaeological record could reveal more than it had before—for instance, as mentioned before, how careful analyses could indicate the presence of particular aspects of social organization such as residence rules. While these studies were important in pointing out the promise of the new approach, the broader promise of building new theory remained largely unfulfilled. There were exceptions, of course, such as Binford's own attempt (in 1968) to explain the rise of agriculture in his article "Post-Pleistocene Adaptations," but by and large little emerged in the way of new laws of culture. While it probably was unfair of the field to expect such quick results, the writings and presentations of some processual archaeologists certainly fueled unrealistic expectations.

The field also got caught up in another issue, which ultimately turned out to be less critical for the development of the field than seemed to be the case at the time. This issue involved the philosophy of science in general and, more specifically, the nature of explanation. Some New Archaeologists urged that archaeologists should use strict deductive procedures in explaining the past. In its most simple form, the New Archaeological argument was that traditional archaeology moved from the specific to the general and followed inductive procedures, while processual archaeology should deduce specific expectations from general theory. According to this position, archaeologists should principally be concerned with *testing* general theories against the archaeological record.

These assertions proved quite contentious for a number of reasons. First, they ignored many of the problems involved in interpreting the archaeological record. By their very nature, specific archaeological interpretations of the record most often involve analogies and are therefore *inductive* rather than *deductive*. So, no matter how explanations are tested, some part of the interpretive procedure has to be inductive.

Second, the scholars who urged the adoption of a deductive stance did not put their assertions in the context of the ongoing debates in the philosophy of science over the question of explanatory procedures. Rather than review the variety of alternative positions and discuss their strengths and weaknesses, processual archaeologists at the time tended to assert, both formally and informally, that there was one acceptable version of explanatory procedures.

Third, the proponents of strict deductive procedures did not successfully grapple with the problem of building new general theories in the absence of existing ones. Since one could not deduce the theoretical expectations to be tested in the absence of a general theory from which such expectations could be deduced, in retrospect more attention should have been paid to theory building. While these philosophical debates in practice were very healthy and certainly helped bring important issues under explicit scrutiny, they had the negative effect of turning some archaeologists away from processual archaeology.

Thus, by the early to mid-1970s, processual archaeology was having growth pains. Although Binford had been remarkably successful in convincing the field of both the problems with the traditional normative approach and the promise of the new systemic one, the initial bloom had begun to fade. While many archaeologists felt they could see where the discipline should be heading, it still was not clear *how* it could successfully achieve the goal of explaining cultural processes.

Rethinking the New Archaeology

Perhaps the most momentous development at the end of what Gordon Willey and I have called the first phase of processual archaeology did not occur in reaction to Binford's writings but happened in Binford's own thinking, as well as that of some of his colleagues and students.

By the beginning of the 1970s, Binford realized that he needed to concentrate on the specific means that archaeologists use to interpret the archaeological record if the New Archaeology was going to be able to build a theoretical understanding of culture change. In so doing, he identified a major methodological flaw in his earlier arguments. Previously, he had urged archaeologists to reverse the traditional contention that by building up a descriptive, historical understanding of the past, questions of cultural process could be confronted. Instead, he had advocated a new paradigm—one that maintained that only with an understanding of cultural processes could culture histories be constructed. What he realized, however, was that in order to create new insights into cultural processes, archaeologists also had to challenge the assumptions that even processual archaeologists themselves were making about the archaeological record.

While some processual archaeologists, most notably Michael B. Schiffer, successfully broached this topic by concentrating in innovative ways on the physical creation of the archaeological record, Binford, in a series of publications in the 1970s and 1980s, focused his attention more generally on the most critical aspect of archaeological interpretation: *analogies*, the logical procedure whereby similarities in specifics are used to infer similarities in general. He contrasted the static record of the present—what scholars study today—with the dynamic behaviors of the past that helped produce the record. The key problem, he argued, was linking the activities of the past with the archaeological record that survives in the modern world. Binford termed this linkage "giving meaning to the record." Making such linkages had been an essential part of archaeological interpretation since the beginnings of the discipline. But Binford challenged the haphazard way in which these interpretations had been made and the frequent lack of justification or verification of the suggested linkages.

To give a simple example, archaeologists uncovering a large rectangle of stones might make the inference that they had found the remains of a perishable structure. This inference might be based on an analogy to modern wood-and-thatch structures that have a single row of stones to support the wooden walls at their bases. The presence of a burned area inside the stone perimeter might strengthen the archaeologists' confidence in the initial inference and might lead to further inferences, also based on analogies, that the burned area was a hearth and the structure was a house. After subsequently finding a number of similar remains, the archaeologists might talk about having located a village, although they actually had only discovered a series of patterned remains. Through time, the original analogy-based inference might be forgotten, with the inference becoming an unchallenged assumption. Binford asserted that similar chains of reasoning occurred in the field for much more complex inferences, as well.

Binford realized that more reliable inferential procedures for giving meaning to the record needed to be developed. He called for the growth of what he termed "middle-range theory" (in retrospect, a confusing term), or "bridging theory," to consistently link regular behaviors and patterning in the archaeological record. In order to achieve such linkages, Binford turned to the nascent methodology of ethnoarchaeology. In this latter approach, archaeologists undertake ethnographic research themselves, instead of relying on cultural anthropological colleagues, who often do not provide the kinds of data on material culture that archaeologists need. A general goal of ethnoarchaeological research is to examine modern people in order to relate their activities (such as kinds of hunting) to the patterned material consequences of their behaviors. If similar artifactual patterns are found in the archaeological record and the parameters (such as environmental factors) in both cases can be substantially controlled, then the inference that the modern behaviors and the ancient ones are similar would have strong support (although it would not be completely verified). Furthermore, if the inference can be generalized over a series of cases, then a "bridging theory" linking behavior and record might be established.

Following the lead of ethnoarchaeological pioneers such as Patty Jo Watson, Binford shifted his own research agenda to the study of modern peoples. He undertook fieldwork with the Nunamiut Eskimos with the goals of understanding their mobile lifeway, particularly as regards food procurement; learning about the material consequences of their varied hunting activities over a full calendar cycle; uncovering possible patterning in such consequences; and finding out why this patterning occurs.

The links between the behavioral patterns (related to hunting activities, for example) and the material patterns (such as hunting stands located in particular places and used at specific times of the year) might then serve as the bases for various archaeological research strategies. These could be directed toward finding environmental and cultural parameters of past cultures that were similar to the ethnographic case; identifying the locations and kinds of archaeological situations where appropriate material remains might be found; and seeing if patterns that were similar to the ethnographic ones appeared. If such patterns did appear, then the archaeologist would be in a position to make an analogical inference between the ethnographic and archaeological cases that hopefully would shed light on both the nature of and reasons for ancient behaviors that archaeologists, unlike ethnographers, cannot directly observe.

There were other strategic implications in the new methodological directions that Binford and others began explicitly to espouse in the 1970s. Paramount among them was the shift in research procedures. Instead of most analyses occurring after archaeological field research had been undertaken, the new middle-range approach called for significant research and analyses—utilizing ethnoarchaeological findings along with existing scholarship—*before* the start of archaeological fieldwork, so that archaeologists would not be initiating their archaeological field research without the background needed to organize efficient and productive fieldwork strategies. Clearly such new procedures had important consequences for a variety of issues, including funding (for research preceding the archaeological fieldwork); the time needed for a project; and the scale of projects, which would not necessarily be limited to single archaeological sites.

The ultimate expectation and hope of Binford and like-minded colleagues was that as the meanings given to the archaeological record became regularized through time, archaeologists would be more able to build theories that could in turn be tested against a meaningful archaeological record. The middle-range emphasis in the processual approach helped revitalize it after the initial polemical onslaught had begun to wane and reconfirmed Binford's continuing intellectual leadership in archaeological theory and method. Although serious philosophical questions about the middle-range approach still remain, it continues to be an important intellectual stimulus to the field of archaeology today. Moreover, unlike the traditional culture-historical emphasis on data gathering before theory formation, the attention of processual archaeologists to *specific* bridging arguments does not appear to have deflected interest in the field away from more *general* theory building. Rather, the specific concerns currently seem to be stimulating the broader ones.

Binford's Legacy

Despite dire predictions and pronouncements to the contrary, processual archaeology appears to be thriving. While attacks from so-called postprocessualists continue, the tradition Lewis Binford initiated shows continuing vitality. In part, this is due to new insights and understandings of the development of human culture through time and space from hunters and gatherers to complex civilization. It is also due to the adaptability processualism has shown in recent years. For instance, part of the postprocessual critique has centered on the New Archaeology's preoccupation with the technoenvironmental realm. While Binford has written about the importance of all aspects of the cultural system, in practice, processual archaeologists (Binford included), by and large, have ignored the realm of religion and ideology. But this one-sidedness is changing as processual archaeology has broadened its outlook and is now coming closer to Binford's original conception.

While the tangible results of processual archaeology have been substantial, perhaps the most lasting contributions, which Lewis Binford made more than three decades ago and which form a key component of his continuing legacy for the field of archaeology, are the boundless optimism that he helped instill in the field and the ongoing intellectual ferment that he first stirred. Archaeology has not been the same since Binford's 1962 article, and the current positive trajectory of the discipline, its popularity, and its immense productivity owe much to Lewis Binford's stimulating research, teaching, and publication.

APPENDIX

A BRIEF SUMMARY OF LEWIS R. BINFORD'S FIELD RESEARCH

See Binford's three volumes of collected essays—*An Archaeological Perspective* (1972), *Working at Archaeology* (1983), and *Debating Archaeology* (1989)—as well as his general book *In Pursuit of the Past: Decoding the Archaeological Record* (1983) for further discussions of his fieldwork and its relation to his intellectual development.

North Carolina and Virginia (1956–1957)

Binford undertook both archaeological and ethnohistoric research, concentrating in coastal zones. This work resulted in his 1964 doctoral dissertation at the University of Michigan: *Archaeological and Ethnohistorical Investigation of Cultural Diversity and Progressive Development among Aboriginal Cultures of Coastal Virginia and North Carolina*. It also led to a long-term interest in historical archaeology, which in turn led to some important articles, including a short but oft-cited 1962 piece ("A New Method of Calculating Dates from Kaolin Pipe Stem Samples") that used a statistical analysis to date the remains of pipes found in historic sites.

Michigan (1958–1961)

Binford helped direct archaeological surveys and excavations as part of a University of Michigan project in 1958 and 1960 and worked at the historic site of Fort Michilimackinac in 1959 and 1961 as assistant field director and then director of excavations. Some of the results of the latter project were published in a 1961 monograph, *Excavations at Fort Michilimackinac*, by Moreau S. Maxwell and Lewis R. Binford. Binford's other archaeological research in Michigan helped coalesce many of his early ideas about the problems with traditional archaeological approaches and the means to challenge them. Binford's first pathbreaking article, "Archaeology as Anthropology," which appeared in *American Antiquity* in 1962, immediately followed these field activities. This fieldwork also resulted in a series of site reports and articles on such topics as stone tool manufacture, which became a lifelong interest of Binford. In addition, the important 1963 article on "Red Ocher Caches from the Michigan Area: A Possible Case of Cultural Drift" derived from the Michigan research.

Illinois (1962–1963)

Binford directed an archaeological project for the National Park Service in an area near the construction of the Carlyle Reservoir Dam. This field research resulted in the publication of one of the first "New Archaeology" site reports: *Archaeology at Hatchery West* (1970), by Lewis R. Binford, Sally R. Binford, Robert Whallon, and Margaret Ann Hardin, which was published by the Society for American Archaeology. This Illinois research made important methodological contributions to the field, particularly as regards growing recognition of activity differentiation and the structure of archaeological sites. It also stimulated Binford's thinking about the sampling of archaeological sites ("A Consideration of Archaeological Research Design," published in 1964) and archaeologists' employment of ethnographic analogies ("Smudge Pits and Hide Smoking: The Use of Analogy in Archaeological Reasoning," published in 1967).

Southwest France (1968–1969)

Working with Sally R. Binford and building on prior visits to French sites, Binford launched his ongoing analyses of previously excavated materials from Combe Grenal and cemented a new interest in the Paleolithic Mousterian culture, an interest that has continued unabated to the present. He challenged traditional typological views of Mousterian tools and set forth new ideas about varied Mousterian cultural activities and their consequences for the appearance and structure of the archaeological record. Chapters 8-16 of *Working at Archaeology* present some of Binford's principal papers on the Mousterian.

Nunamiut, Anaktuvuk Pass, Alaska (1969, 1971–1972)

In the late 1960s, Binford realized that he had to address the methodological quandary of how to link the static archaeological record that researchers view today with the dynamic cultural activities of the past that helped produce the modern record. He also came to understand, as had other archeologists of the period, that archaeologists could not rely on cultural anthropologists, who as a whole had lost interest in everyday material culture, to produce data about such links. Therefore, following the lead of several pioneering colleagues such as Patty Jo Watson, he undertook ethnographic research among the Nunamiut peoples of Alaska. He concentrated his attention on certain activities, such as caribou hunting, that had useful implications for the formation of the archaeological record and showed how his modern study might help give meaning to patterns that archaeologists found in impermanent hunter-gatherer sites they were investigating. Binford's research resulted in the influential book *Nunamiut Ethnoarchaeology* (1978) and several important articles, including "Forty-seven Trips: A Case Study in the Character of Some Formation Processes" (1976), "Dimensional

Analysis of Behavior and Site Structure: Learning from an Eskimo Hunting Squad" (1978), and "Willow Smoke and Dogs' Tails: Hunter-Gatherer Settlement Systems and Archaeological Site Formation" (1980). In addition, Binford's work on comparisons between the marks left on animal bones by humans and wolves is discussed in the 1981 book *Bones: Ancient Men and Modern Myths*, which is also largely derived from his Nunamiut research.

Alyawara Speakers, Central Australia (1974)

Binford continued his ethnoarchaeological research on modern hunter-gatherer peoples by undertaking studies in Australia in cooperation with the archaeologist James O'Connell. This inquiry resulted in three detailed articles on "An Alyawara Day," published between 1984 and 1986, all of which have important methodological value.

South Africa (1981)

During a visit to South Africa, Binford was able to combine laboratory and museum studies with brief field studies of animal behavior and bone taphonomy. This African work resulted in his 1984 book on *Faunal Remains from Klasies River Mouth* as well as a 1988 coauthored article on hyena scavenging behavior and also furthered his publications relating to the ongoing scholarly debates about human origins.

China (1985)

A research trip to China in the mid-1980s allowed Binford to examine collections and sites there. This research has influenced his writings on site structure and comparisons between early hominids and *Homo sapiens* (see, for example, his 1989 article on "Isolating the Transition to Cultural Adaptations: An Organizational Approach") and also led to reexaminations of well-known sites such as Zhoukoudian (see Lewis R. Binford and Nancy M. Stone, "Zhoukoudian: A Closer Look," 1986).

Binford is currently synthesizing his long-term studies of hunter-gatherer peoples, both past and present, for a major comparative book on mobile adaptations through time and space.

SELECT BIBLIOGRAPHY OF LEWIS R. BINFORD'S WORKS

[Moreau S. Maxwell and Lewis R. Binford] *Excavations at Fort Michilimackinac*. Contributions in Anthropology 1(1), Michigan State University, East Lansing (1961).

"Archaeology as Anthropology," *American Antiquity* 28:217–225 (1962).

"A New Method of Calculating Dates from Kaolin Pipe Stem Samples," *Southeastern Archaeological Conference Newsletter* 9:19–25 (1962).

"Red Ocher Caches from the Michigan Area: A Possible Case of Cultural Drift," *Southwestern Journal of Anthropology* 19:89–108 (1963).

"A Consideration of Archaeological Research Design," *American Antiquity* 29:425–441 (1964).

Archaeological and Ethnohistorical Investigation of Cultural Diversity and Progressive Development among Aboriginal Cultures of Coastal Virginia and North Carolina. University Microfilms, Ann Arbor (1964). [Reprinted in 1991 by Garland Publishing Company.]

"Archaeological Systematics and the Study of Culture Process," *American Antiquity* 31:203–210 (1965).

"Smudge Pits and Hide Smoking: The Use of Analogy in Archaeological Reasoning," *American Antiquity* 32:1–12 (1967).

[Sally R. Binford and Lewis R. Binford, editors] *New Perspectives in Archeology*. Aldine, Chicago (1968).

"Post-Pleistocene Adaptations," in *New Perspectives in Archeology*, edited by S. R. Binford and L. R. Binford, pp. 313–341. Aldine, Chicago (1968).

[Lewis R. Binford, Sally R. Binford, Robert Whallon, and Margaret Ann Hardin] *Archaeology at Hatchery West*. Memoirs of the Society for American Archaeology 24 (1970).

An Archaeological Perspective. Seminar Press, New York (1972).

"Forty-seven Trips: A Case Study in the Character of Some Formation Processes," in *Contributions to Anthropology: The Interior Peoples of Northern Alaska*, edited by E. S. Hall, Jr., pp. 249–351. Mercury Series, Paper 49. National Museum of Canada, National Museum of Man, Ottawa (1976).

"General Introduction," in *For Theory Building in Archaeology: Essays on Faunal Remains, Aquatic Resources, Spatial Analysis and Systemic Modeling*, edited by L. R. Binford, pp. 1–10. Academic Press, New York (1977).

"Dimensional Analysis of Behavior and Site Structure: Learning from an Eskimo Hunting Stand," *American Antiquity* 43:330–361 (1978).

Nunamiut Ethnoarchaeology. Academic Press, New York (1978).

"Willow Smoke and Dogs' Tails: Hunter-Gatherer Settlement Systems and Archaeological Site Formation," *American Antiquity* 45:4–20 (1980).

Bones: Ancient Men and Modern Myths. Academic Press, New York (1981).

In Pursuit of the Past: Decoding the Archaeological Record. Thames and Hudson, London (1983).

Working at Archaeology. Academic Press, New York (1983).

"An Alyawara Day: Flour, Spinifex Gum, and Shifting Perspectives," *Journal of Anthropological Research* 40:157–182 (1984).

[Lewis R. Binford and James F. O'Connell] "An Alyawara Day: The Stone Quarry," *Journal of Anthropological Research* 40:406–432 (1984).

Faunal Remains from Klasies River Mouth. Academic Press, Orlando (1984).

"An Alyawara Day: Making Men's Knives and Beyond," *American Antiquity* 51:547–562 (1986).

[Lewis R. Binford and Nancy M. Stone] "Zhoukoudian: A Closer Look," *Current Anthropology* 27:453–476 (1986).

[Lewis R. Binford, M. G. L. Mills, and Nancy M. Stone] "Hyena Scavenging Behavior and Its Implications for the Interpretation of Faunal Assemblages from FLK 22 (the Zinj Floor) at Olduvai Gorge," *Journal of Anthropological Archaeology* 7:99–135 (1988).

Debating Archaeology. Academic Press, San Diego (1989).

"Isolating the Transition to Cultural Adaptations: An Organizational Approach," in *The Emergence of Modern Human: Biocultural Adaptations in the Later Pleistocene,* edited by Erik Trinkaus, pp. 18–41. Cambridge University Press, Cambridge (1989).

"Mobility, Housing, and Environment: A Comparative Study," *Journal of Anthropological Research* 46:119–152 (1990).

"Is Australian Site Structure Explained by the Absence of Predators?" *Journal of Anthropological Achaeology* 10:255:282 (1991).

SUGGESTED READINGS, INCLUDING MAJOR WRITINGS BY ANTHROPOLOGISTS AND ARCHAEOLOGISTS MENTIONED IN THE TEXT

Aberle, David F. *The Psychosocial Analysis of a Hopi Life-History.* University of California Press, Berkeley (1951).

Adams, Robert McC. "Some Hypotheses on the Development of Early Civilizations," *American Antiquity* 21:227–232 (1956).

———. *The Evolution of Urban Society: Early Mesopotamia and Prehispanic Mexico.* Aldine, Chicago (1966).

Binford, Sally R. "Variability and Change in Near Eastern Mousterian of Levallois Facies," in *New Perspectives in Archeology*, edited by Sally R. Binford and Lewis R. Binford, pp. 49–60. Aldine, Chicago (1968).

Bordes, François. *The Old Stone Age.* McGraw-Hill, New York (1968).

———. *A Tale of Two Caves.* Harper and Row, New York (1972).

Braidwood, Robert J. *The Near East and the Foundations for Civilization.* Condon Lectures. Oregon State System for Higher Education, Eugene (1952).

———. "Archaeology and the Evolutionary Theory," in *Evolution and Anthropology: A Centennial Appraisal*, edited by B. J. Meggers, pp. 76–89. Anthropological Society of Washington, D.C. (1959).

Caldwell, Joseph R. *Trend and Tradition in the Prehistory of the Eastern United States.* Illinois State Museum Scientific Papers 10, and the American Anthropological Association Memoir 88, Springfield and Menasha, Wisconsin (1958).

———. "The New American Archaeology," *Science* 129 (3345): 303–307 (1959).

Campbell, John M. "Territoriality among Ancient Hunters: Interpretations from Ethnography and Nature," in *Anthropological Archaeology in the Americas*, edited by B. J. Meggers, pp. 1–21. Anthropological Society of Washington, D.C. (1968).

Clarke, David L. *Analytical Archaeology*. Methuen, London (1968).

Coe, Joffre L. *The Formative Cultures of the Carolina Piedmont*. Transactions of the American Philosophical Society 54 (5), Philadelphia (1964).

Cole, Fay-Cooper, and Thorne Deuel. *Rediscovering Illinois*. University of Chicago Press, Chicago (1937).

Courbin, Paul. *What Is Archaeology? An Essay on the Nature of Archaeological Research*. University of Chicago Press, Chicago (1988).

DeJarnette, David L., and S. B. Wimberly. *The Bessemer Site*. Geological Survey of Alabama, Museum Paper 17. University of Alabama, Tuscaloosa (1941).

Eggan, Fred. *Social Organization of the Western Pueblos*. University of Chicago Press, Chicago (1950).

Ellis, Florence Hawley. *Reconstruction of the Basic Jemez Pattern of Social Organization*. University of New Mexico Press, Albuquerque (1964).

Embree, Lester (editor). *Metaarchaeology: Reflections by Archaeologists and Philosophers*. Boston Series in the Philosophy of Science, Vol. 147. Kluwer Academic Publishers, Dordrecht (1992).

Flannery, Kent V. "Archaeological Systems Theory and Early Mesoamerica," in *Anthropological Archaeology in the Americas*, edited by B. J. Meggers, pp. 67–87. Anthropological Society of Washington, D.C. (1968).

———. "The Cultural Evolution of Civilizations," *Annual Review of Ecology and Systematics* 3:399–426 (1972).

Ford, James A. "On the Concept of Types," *American Anthropologist* 56:42–53 (1954).

———. *A Quantitative Method for Deriving Cultural Chronology*. Pan American Union, Technical Manual 1. Washington, D.C. (1962).

Greenman, Emerson F. *The Younge Site*. University of Michigan, Museum of Anthropology, Occasional Contributions 6. Ann Arbor (1937).

Griffin, James B. *The Fort Ancient Aspect: Its Cultural and Chronological Position in Mississippi Valley Archaeology*. University of Michigan Press, Ann Arbor (1943).

———. "Eastern North American Archaeology: A Summary," *Science* 156 (3772): 175–191 (1967).

Hawkes, Christopher F. C. "Archaeological Theory and Method: Some Suggestions from the Old World," *American Anthropologist* 56:155–168 (1954).

Hill, James N. "A Prehistoric Community in Eastern Arizona," *Southwestern Journal of Anthropology* 22:9–30 (1966).

Hodder, Ian. *Reading the Past*, second edition. Cambridge University Press, Cambridge (1991).

Howell, F. Clark, and François Bouiliere (editors). *African Ecology and Human Evolution*. Aldine, Chicago (1963).

Isaac, Glynn L., assisted by Barbara Isaac. *Olorgesailie: Archaeological Studies of a Middle Pleistocene Lake Basin in Kenya*. University of Chicago Press, Chicago (1977).

Kroeber, Alfred L. *Cultural and Natural Areas of Native North America*. University of California Publications in American Archaeology and Ethnology 38, Berkeley (1939).

———. *Anthropology*. Harcourt, Brace, and World, New York (1948).

Leone, Mark P. (editor). *Contemporary Archaeology*. Southern Illinois University Press, Carbondale (1972).

Lewis, Thomas M. N., and Madeline Kneberg. *Hiwassee Island: An Archaeological Account of Four Tennessee Indian Peoples*. University of Tennessee Press, Knoxville (1946).

Linton, Ralph. *The Study of Man*. Appleton-Century, New York (1936).

———. "North American Cooking Pots," *American Antiquity* 9:369–380 (1944).

Longacre, William A. "Archaeology as Anthropology: A Case Study," *Science* 144 (3625): 1454–1455 (1964).

MacNeish, Richard S. "Ancient Mesoamerican Civilization," *Science* 143 (3606): 531–537 (1964).

Martin, Paul S. "The Revolution in Archaeology," *American Antiquity* 36:1–8 (1971).

Mead, Margaret. *Coming of Age in Samoa*. W. Morrow, New York (1928).

———. *Blackberry Winter: My Earlier Years*. W. Morrow, New York (1972).

Moore, James A., and Arthur S. Keene (editors). *Archaeological Hammers and Theories*. Academic Press, New York (1983).

Movius, Hallam L. "Old World Archaeology: Paleolithic." *Anthropology Today*, edited by A. L. Kroeber, pp. 163–192. University of Chicago Press, Chicago (1953).

———. "Old World Paleolithic." In *Anthropology Today: Selections*, edited by Sol Tax, pp. 122–151. University of Chicago Press, Chicago (1962).

——— (general editor and director of excavations). *Excavation of the Abri Pataud, Les Eyzies (Dordogne)*. Bulletin of the American School of Prehistoric Research 30. Peabody Museum, Harvard University, Cambridge (1975).

O'Connell, James. *The Prehistory of Surprise Valley*. Ballena Press, Ramona, Calif. (1975).

Preucel, Robert W. (editor). *Processual and Postprocessual Archaeologies: Multiple Ways of Knowing the Past*. Center for Archaeological Investigations, Southern Illinois University at Carbondale (1991).

Radcliffe-Brown, A. R. *Structure and Function in Primitive Society*. Free Press, Glencoe (1952).

Redman, Charles L., Mary Jane Berman, Edward V. Curtin, William T. Langhorne, Jr., Nina M. Versaggi, and Jeffrey C. Wanser (editors). *Social Archaeology: Beyond Subsistence and Dating*. Academic Press, New York (1978).

Renfrew, Colin. "An Interview with Lewis Binford." *Current Anthropology* 28:683–694 (1987).

Sabloff, Jeremy A. "When the Rhetoric Fades: A Brief Appraisal of Intellectual Trends in American Archaeology during the Past Two Decades," *Bulletin of the Schools of Oriental Research* 242:1–6 (1982).

Salmon, Merrilee H. *Philosophy and Archaeology*. Academic Press, New York (1982).

Saxe, Arthur A. "Social Dimensions of Mortuary Practice in a Mesolithic Population from Wadi Halfa, Sudan," in *Approaches to the Social Dimensions of Mortuary Practices*, edited by James A. Brown, pp. 39–57. Memoirs of the Society for American Archaeology 25 (1971).

Schiffer, Michael B. *Behavioral Archaeology*. Academic Press, New York (1976).

Service, Elman R. *Primitive Social Organization*. Random House, New York (1962).

———. *Origins of the State and Civilization*. Norton, New York (1975).

Shanks, Michael, and Christopher Tilley. *Re-constructing Archaeology: Theory and Practice*, second edition. Routledge, London (1992).

South, Stanley A. "Evolutionary Theory in Archaeology," *Southern Indian Studies* 7:10–32 (1955).

———. *Method and Theory in Historical Archaeology*. Academic Press, New York (1977).

Spaulding, Albert C. "Statistical Techniques for the Discovery of Artifact Types," *American Antiquity* 18:305–313 (1953).

———. "The Dimensions of Archaeology," in *Essays in the Science of Culture*, edited by Gertrude E. Dole and Robert L. Carneiro, pp. 437–456. Crowell, New York (1960).

Spuhler, James N., et al. *The Evolution of Man's Capacity for Culture*. Wayne State University Press, Detroit (1957).

Steward, Julian H. "Ecological Aspects of Southwestern Society," *Anthropos* 32:87–104 (1937).

———. *Theory of Culture Change*. University of Illinois Press, Urbana (1955).

Struever, Stuart, and Gail Houart. "An Analysis of the Hopewell Interaction Sphere," in *Social Exchange and Interaction*, edited by E. Wilmsen, pp. 47–80. Museum of Anthropology, University of Michigan, Ann Arbor (1972).

Tax, Sol (editor). *Evolution after Darwin: The University of Chicago Centennial*. University of Chicago Press, Chicago (1960).

Taylor, Walter W. *A Study of Archaeology*. Memoirs of the American Anthropological Association, No. 69 (1948). [Reprinted by the Center for Archaeological Investigations, Southern Illinois University at Carbondale (1983).]

Trigger, Bruce D. *A History of Archaeological Thought*. Cambridge University Press, Cambridge (1989).

Wandsnider, LuAnn (editor). *Quandaries and Quests: Visions of Archaeology's Future*. Center for Archaeological Investigations, Southern Illinois University at Carbondale (1992).

Watson, Patty Jo. *Archaeological Ethnography in Western Iran*. University of Arizona Press, Tucson (1979).

Watson, Patty Jo, Steven A. LeBlanc, and Charles L. Redman. *Explanation in Archaeology: An Explicitly Scientific Approach*. Columbia University Press, New York (1971).

Wauchope, Robert. *Archaeological Survey of Northern Georgia*. Memoirs of the Society for American Archaeology 21 (1966).

White, Leslie A. *The Science of Culture: A Study of Man and Civilization*. Farrar, Straus, New York (1949).

———. *The Evolution of Culture*. McGraw-Hill, New York (1959).

Williams, B. J. *A Model of Band Society*. Memoirs of the Society for American Archaeology 29 (1974).

Willey, Gordon R. *Prehistoric Settlement Patterns in the Viru Valley, Peru*. Bureau of American Ethnology Bulletin 155, Washington, D.C. (1953).

Willey, Gordon R., and Philip Phillips. *Method and Theory in American Archaeology*. University of Chicago Press, Chicago (1958).

Willey, Gordon R., and Jeremy A. Sabloff. *A History of American Archaeology*, third edition. W. H. Freeman, New York (1993).

Winters, Howard Dalton. *The Riverton Culture: A Second Millennium Occupation in the Central Wabash Valley*. Illinois State Museum and the Illinois Archaeological Survey, Springfield (1969).

Wylie, Alison. "The Interpretive Dilemma," in *Critical Traditions in Contemporary Archaeology*, edited by V. Pinsky and A. Wylie, pp. 18–27. Cambridge Unversity Press, Cambridge (1989).